THE
SPIRITUAL ASPECTS
OF THE NEW POETRY

The
Spiritual Aspects
of the New Poetry

by

AMOS N. WILDER

Essay Index Reprint Series

BOOKS FOR LIBRARIES PRESS
FREEPORT, NEW YORK

LIBRARY OF CONGRESS CATALOG CARD NUMBER:

68-16988

PRINTED IN THE UNITED STATES OF AMERICA

To

CATHARINE

CONTENTS

PREFACE

The field of contemporary poetry taken in all its variety offers an extraordinary interest to those concerned with values or who are in the best sense of the term moralists. Moreover, most of the chief types of perennial religious impulse are to be found here, and found in revealing relationship to present-day society. This literature offers itself both as a criticism of life today and as a testimony to life today, and because it is poetry its criticism and its testimony are of fundamental character. Here is a mirror in which the world can know itself and in which it can read its deepest dilemmas and its deepest omens.

Yet while the more strictly literary aspects of this field have been studied, there has been strangely little scrutiny of its spiritual aspects apart from some passing comment in critical essays. And these tentatives toward a general interpretation have been made almost exclusively by writers closely identified with the modernist movement in literature. It is high time that those who count themselves traditionalists in the best sense of the term should give to this rich body of material some of the same assessment and discernment that the contemporary novel has received.

Primary place must be given in any such consideration of contemporary poetry to work of nontraditional character, to work of the last two decades which is experimental or rebellious as judged by the standards before that time. I was one of those who had little acquaintance with

the many forms of "modern" poetry until a dozen years
ago. I did not know until I read it that it was concerned
with matters important to me that were largely untouched
in traditional poetry. I found that some of my own auto-
biography was recorded in these poets and that I knew
myself and my age better for having read them. No doubt
there was much that was alien to me, and no doubt I
came out at a different point from most of these writers.
Yet in many respects they were writing about the world I
lived in more truly than poets of the traditional schools.
These varieties of contemporary poetry must receive large
place if we hope to find in it a full criticism of and a full
testimony to our age. Indeed, the present study largely
limits itself to these groups, partly because the outlook of
the traditional poetry is generally understood, and partly
because the new poets speak more immediately out of the
moods of our day.

Three particular interests have defined themselves in
the study of these poets and in the formulation of this
book. I have been interested, first of all, in finding what
light the new poetry throws upon the religious and ethical
attitudes of men today, especially those not identified with
the older traditions. What do twentieth century men live
by? What are their values? What do they think of life?
Which way are they moving? How does secularism, how
does paganism (if such it is) speak when its bars are
down? The poets should be to some degree representative.

But there is a second interest to which considerable
space is given, an interest not so obvious in the title. Given
these attitudes, these features of the new poetry, what is
their soil? What light is thrown on contemporary culture

and social conditions by these findings? What factors evidently determine or influence the world view of our poets? If there is widespread negation not to say spiritual demoralization, does it point to a corresponding disarray in the times? If we find vehement protest, ethically grounded, against aspects of modern life, are the poets to be reckoned dependable analysts, as dependable, say, as social scientists? May we not, indeed, anticipate that the poets will guide us to exceptionally precise and profound understanding of the maladies of our world? Whether they are afflicted or not? Perhaps the more cogently if they, too, are afflicted? In the area of this second interest I have been led inevitably to adduce parallels or comments from novelist and critic.

I have been interested, in the third place, in assessing the outlook of these poets and those among moderns for whom they speak. I have sought to understand the context out of which their negations and affirmations spring and to do justice to the various attitudes and values discovered, and yet at the same time I have not hesitated to mark those points at which the new poets pass into unreality, irresponsibility or error. Nor have I hesitated to pass judgment on the traditionalist whether in his poetry or in his outlook as a whole.

In either case the standpoint adopted as a basis for criticism is the Christian tradition. This tradition is understood in terms neither of Catholic nor Protestant orthodoxy, neither of Puritanism nor humanism, but in terms of what has been called classical Christianity. By this is meant Christianity in its creative as opposed to its ossified moments and aspects. The creative aspect has never been totally absent, neither do I mean to exclude doctrinal and institutional developments when I speak of creative aspects. But the Christian tradition is most profoundly disclosed in the New Testament, in certain moments and figures of the Catholic Church, Orthodox and Latin, and in the initiatory phases and essential motives of the Reformation. The Reformation entered into disappointing combinations with the human material and national characteristics of the peoples it conquered and it brought with it a regrettable carry-over from the Middle Ages. But its profounder impulses set mighty creative forces in movement, and in particular set their stamp upon the Anglo-Saxon and especially the American character. This is "the pit from which we were digged." The Christian tradition in its Reformation expression is, therefore, the one most relevant and illuminating for our situation. In particular, it is here that we find the sanction for our Anglo-Saxon and American norm of autonomous, responsible personality, a norm as decisive for our political and social as for our religious outlook. It is this norm that serves me constantly in the following pages as a touchstone for the condemnation of either individualism and romantic subjectivism on the one hand or collectivism on the other, both of which have luxuriant manifestations in the new poetry. The peculiar ills of contemporary life and of contemporary artists can only be clearly challenged by confrontation with the Christian emphasis on personality and the responsible self.

My early chapters will make clear that the writers I am here mainly concerned with as the "new poets" are those often called "modernist" or "experimental," those who at

one or more points are in revolt against the Victorian or
Georgian tradition. They have their fellows in all the arts
today, and those versed in modernist painting or music
should be able to identify corresponding phenomena in
those arts. By directing my study especially to this group
I do not mean to belittle the poets of today writing in
more traditional ways and with usually more positive outlook. Nor do I share except in part the widespread reaction of the modernists against the Victorian and Georgian
poets. It is my view, however, that the world today is
passing through a crisis of such exceptional character that
those artists who speak out of it have a peculiar significance, whether in the long run they be counted of permanent value or not.

I have not proposed here to deal with all the modernist
poets, nor even with all the important ones. Nor have I
sought to give a complete account of the work of those
specially noted. The particular interests indicated have
only required that the work in this field should be noted
where it touches most directly upon matters of faith and
negation. The poets or subject matter here presented may
be viewed as representative rather than exhaustive. It is
clear that even a limited examination of post-war poetry
and criticism discloses highly significant attitudes for those
interested in social trends and in what we may call in the
largest sense religious values.

In connection with the three interests noted above, I
have had it in mind also that there were many people of
supposed conservative tastes and acquaintance in poetry
who would welcome some exposition of the newer work
by one of their own number. Such readers should recog-

nize, however, that this work is not easy to understand and enjoy, and for different reasons in different cases. It has a fairly long tradition of development behind it, but one that is largely outside the tradition of English poetry with which they are acquainted. It is the work in some cases of peculiarly sophisticated and subtle minds or of men deeply versed in special areas of contemporary experience. For the benefit of such readers not fully initiated into modernist poetry I have sought to include brief explanation as to the figures or works named in the text or footnotes, but they are especially referred to the section in the appendix, *Orientation and Reading Guide,* for fuller introduction. It is hoped that Part I of the book itself with its comparison of modernist and traditionalist poetry will serve a similar purpose. The selective classified bibliography is offered as a guide to further reading. Full titles of works mentioned in the book will be found there.

There are a number of things that may be briefly said here on this matter of the difficulty of much recent poetry. Experience shows that new work in the arts, even excellent work, has to make its way against resistance. This does not excuse bad new work, but it leads us to be very careful in rejection of new work that appears strange. Again, when we say that poetry if it is good should make its appeal to "our common intelligence," Laura Riding and Robert Graves ask us if that does not mean "the mind in its least active state."[1] They further query just how far we are right when we say that we understand the older poetry.

[1] *A Survey of Modernist Poetry* (London, 1929). See chapter IV: "The Unpopularity of Modernist Poetry with the Plain Reader." On Riding and Graves see appendix, p. 248.

Do we understand Shakespeare when we read him? Or do
we just read him off the top level? Their most piquant
conclusion is that "the plain reader's approach to poetry
is adequate only for poems as weak as the critical effort
that he is ready to apply to them." We remind the reader
further that he is to be prepared for an elliptical style in
the new work based on the "stream of consciousness" procedure familiar in prose today. Also that there is a small
group of poets who write for their own group rather than
for the general public, and understanding of their work
necessitates explanation. The same would have held true
for a Roman of the time of Domitian who wished to read
the Apocalypse, and is still true for modern readers of
that book. It is useful to bear in mind the violent revulsion
of many against the total cultural scheme of today with its
orthodox art and letters to appreciate the satisfaction many
artists have in finding a new vocabulary and a new
method. There are no doubt some poets who are unintelligible at times through sense of humor, some through
the desire to shock, some through the desire to call attention to themselves. Many are obscure because of their sheer
incompetence to handle the difficult subject matter they
propose. Some are handicapped by neuroses or neurotic
factors. But with all these elements a varied and thrilling
display of human talent manifests itself in this poetry.

It has been part of my purpose here to engage a certain conversation with the new schools of both poets and
critics over issues of ethics and world view that appear
in their work. It is regrettable that so wide a gulf has
existed between the modern artist or writer and the more
alert circles in church and university. Both groups are

concerned with a better design for living than our present
society affords. College and university professors and
theologians have often been uncomprehending and cen-
sorious with regard to new work in the arts. Today, however, it should be possible to find a good deal of common
ground for parley. Thus in addition to scrutiny of the
poetry of today, I have included some discussion of allied
newer movements in criticism. Both the new poetry and
the new criticism evidence attitudes as regards matters of
personal faith which invite comment or query. I have
therefore considered the assumptions as to spiritual or
religious values that appear in the prose criticism of men
like Allen Tate, John Crowe Ransom, Yvor Winters, T. S.
Eliot and others, as well as profited by them at many
points.

In their *Survey of Modernist Poetry* mentioned above,
Laura Riding and Robert Graves have a chapter on "Modernist Poetry and Civilization." The position taken there
is sharply at odds with the approach of this book. They
wish to dissociate poetry from history. They see poets continually plagued by changes in civilization and under
necessity, as the poets think, of responding to it in some
way and so wasting a great deal of energy. "The most in-
telligent attitude toward history is not to take one's own
date too seriously." So they argue that the usual vulgar
sense of modernist, i.e., that which keeps up with the pace
of civilization, is a false ideal for poets. True modernism
"has nothing to do with the date." "Modernist poetry as
such should mean no more than fresh poetry, more poetry,
poetry based on honest invention rather than on conscious imitation of the time spirit." There is much else

in the chapter. In particular one is led to think that what the authors are specially concerned with is the self-consciousness of authors in using the external properties of a new age—trains, dynamos, etc., rather than the deeper issue of the time spirit. Nevertheless, from a point of view concerned with autonomy of art and perhaps, unconfessed, a prejudice against social-ethical themes in poetry, they undercut our present interest in the new poetry. For it is a thesis of this study that our post-war era has a significantly changed spirit and that poetry today serves as an index to it.

There is a real truth in the thesis that art transcends the time and place in which it is created. Insofar as art is concerned with the universal aspects of human nature the statement is evidently correct. Moreover, the achievement of a relative perfection of form, whether by sculpture or the craft of language—apart from the elements that make it up—is something that we lose interest in dating. Artists and poets are well counseled not to be overconscious of such matters as the period in which they work or their national or class affiliations or the movement to which they are supposed to belong. Nevertheless, their work, however general in its concern and appeal, will for observers bear the marks of their setting and illuminate it. Even the greatest creations though they have such a timeless character as to throw into the shade the time relations of their origin do not escape them. But this is even more true of lesser works such as those with which we are here concerned. They are intimately involved in a particular period and time spirit. This is more particularly the case with literature. The arts of language inevitably betray more explicitly than others the conditioning factors, the general assumptions and attitudes of their period and place. As a matter of fact much contemporary poetry frankly devotes itself to the issues of our day.

Again, I question the statement that one's own date in history is to be lightly considered. I have agreed that the artist himself should not be obsessed by it as artist. But the observer and critic has only to gain from a true understanding of the history in the midst of which he and the artist stand. All cultural phenomena take on a greater significance when they are read in the light of their time. Social history has its various phases as does the life of the individual. Some are more significant than others. In the language of today such phases are described in terms of *krisis* and *kairos*. That is, immanent forces that have been working unnoted or obscurely come to a head in social conflict or change. In such hours issues and retributions and perspectives become apparent as they have not before. Are we not living in such a time, and is not the art of such a time significant for the issues that are felt? The words of General Smuts are usually quoted with consent: "There is no doubt that Mankind is once more on the move. The very foundations have been shaken and loosened, and things are again fluid. The tents have been struck, and the great caravan of Mankind is once more on the march." Or one could repeat a passage of Zola cited lately by Mary M. Colum, "We are living in the ruins of a world, our duty is to study the ruins."

I am conscious of a more fundamental query with regard to this project. It will not be raised by those who value the great poetry of the past for its interpretation of life.

But recent literary criticism has been making laudable efforts to draw a clear distinction between poetry as an autonomous discipline and whatever other interests, religion, ethics, sociology, psychology, may find a place in it. All those concerned for clear thinking in aesthetics will approve of this effort. From this point of view the new poets and the new criticism will rightly object to the present approach which looks to art for doctrine, even for didacticism and at worst propaganda. I would try to keep in their good graces, first, by constantly insisting that viewed as *poetry* this material must always first be judged by the aesthetic canons of poetry and not by the alleged superior spirituality or truth of its contents. But we will add that whether for better or worse this poetry abundantly evidences basic viewpoints or convictions. Such data we should be able to use for our purpose, being careful, however, as to how far we identify the particular author under consideration with the given viewpoint.

For stimulus to the particular interests with which this book is concerned I wish to express my appreciation to my sister Charlotte Wilder, also to Georgene and Helen Davis, Herbert Hitchen, Kenneth Patchen and Evelyn Scott. As regards the wider field of poetry in general I am in debt to many others among personal friends, who I trust will find echoes here of their contribution.

ACKNOWLEDGMENTS

The author and publisher acknowledge their indebtedness for permission to quote from the following sources by arrangement with the copyright holders indicated:

Brandt & Brandt for a quotation from *Conversation at Midnight*, by Edna St. Vincent Millay, published by Harper & Brothers, Copyright, 1937 by the author.

The Carnegie Institution for a quotation from *The Vesuvius Eruption of 1906*, by F. A. Perret.

Coward-McCann, Inc. for quotations from *Phases of the Moon*, by Charlotte Wilder, 1936.

Dodd, Mead & Company for quotations from *AE* (George Russell), by Darrell Figgis.

Esprit, Revue Internationale, Paris, for quotations from articles by Jean Bazaine and Charles Plisnier.

Farrar & Rinehart, Inc. for quotations from *Public Speech*, Copyright, 1936 by Archibald MacLeish; and for selections from *The Fall of the City*, a verse play for radio, Copyright, 1937 by Archibald MacLeish, reprinted by permission of Farrar & Rinehart, Inc. Publishers.

Harcourt, Brace & Company, Inc. for quotations from *Poems 1909-1925*, *Murder in the Cathedral*, *The Rock*, and *The Journey of the Magi*, by T. S. Eliot.

Harvard University Press for quotations from papers by Howard Mumford Jones and R. M. MacIver in *Authority and the Individual*, reprinted by permission of the President and Fellows of Harvard College.

Houghton Mifflin Company for quotations from *The Hamlet of A. MacLeish* and *Streets in the Moon*, by Archibald MacLeish.

Liveright Publishing Corporation for a quotation from *The Bridge*, by Hart Crane.

The Macmillan Company for quotations from *Collected Poems by AE*, *Selected Poems*, by T. Sturge Moore, *Songs from the Clay*, by James Stephens, *A Poet's Life*, by Harriet Monroe, *Collected Poems*, by W. B. Yeats, and *Amaranth*, by E. A. Robinson.

New Republic for a quotation from a poem by Archibald Fleming; and for a poem by Eunice Clark reprinted with the authors' permissions.

New Verse, London, for quotations from poems by Kenneth Allot and W. H. Auden, and a prose citation by the editor, Geoffrey Grigson.

The Marchesa Origo for quotations from *Poems*, by Geoffrey Scott.

The Oxford University Press, New York, for a quotation from *Collected Poems*, by W. H. Davies.

The Oxford University Press, London, for a quotation from *Poems*, by G. M. Hopkins.

Kenneth Patchen for extensive quotations from *Before the Brave*.

Librairie Plon, Paris, for quotations from *Un Nouveau Moyen Age*, by Nicolas Berdiaeff.

Ezra Pound for a quotation from his article, "Mang Tsze" in *The Criterion*, London, July 1938.

Random House, Inc. for quotations from the following books reprinted by permission: *On This Island*, by W. H. Auden, 1937; *The Dog Beneath the Skin*, by Auden and

Isherwood, Copyright, 1935, by Modern Library, Inc.; *Before the Brave*, by Kenneth Patchen, Copyright, 1936, by Modern Library, Inc.; *Roan Stallion, Tamar and Other Poems*, by Robinson Jeffers, Copyright, 1925, by Horace Liveright, Inc.; *Cawdor and Other Poems*, by Robinson Jeffers, Copyright, 1928 by Robinson Jeffers; *Give Your Heart to the Hawks*, by Robinson Jeffers, Copyright, 1933, by Random House, Inc.; *The Ascent of F6*, by Auden and Isherwood, Copyright, 1937, by Random House, Inc.; *A New Anthology of Modern Poetry*, by Selden Rodman, Copyright, 1938, by Random House, Inc.; *A Time to Dance*, by C. Day Lewis, Copyright, 1935, by Modern Library, Inc.

Charles Scribner's Sons for quotations from *Selected Poems* and *Preludes for Memnon*, by Conrad Aiken; *The Works of Francis Thompson, The World's Body*, by J. C. Ransom; *Reactionary Essays* and *The Mediterranean and other Poems*, by Allen Tate; and *From These Roots*, by Mary M. Colum.

Evelyn Scott for quotations from *Escapade* and *A Calendar of Sin*.

George N. Shuster for a quotation from his essay "François Mauriac" originally published in *The Bookman*, vol. LXXII, pp. 466-475.

Southern Review for a quotation from an article, "Hulme and the Tragic View," by Dixon Wecter, vol. V, no. 1.

Student World, Geneva for quotations from articles by Nicolas Berdiaeff and Brother George Every.

The Viking Press, Inc. for quotations from *U. S. 1*, by Muriel Rukeyser, Copyright, 1938 by Muriel Rukeyser; *The Collected Poems of D. H. Lawrence, The Letters of*

D. H. Lawrence, Copyright, 1932 by the Estate of D. H. Lawrence; and *A Poet and Two Painters,* by Knud Merrild, reprinted with permission of the Viking Press, Inc.

Yale Review for quotations from the article *Public Speech and Private Speech in Poetry,* by Archibald MacLeish, vol. 27, no. 3.

The Yale University Press for quotations from *Psychology and Religion,* by C. G. Jung.

Yvor Winters and Arrow Editions for quotations from *Primitivism and Decadence,* by Yvor Winters.

PART ONE. MODERNIST AND TRADITIONALIST

No man also having drunk old wine straightway desireth new; for he saith, the old is better.

The world fears a new experience more than it fears anything. Because a new experience displaces so many old experiences. *D. H. Lawrence in conversation.*

Souffrir passe, avoir souffert ne passe jamais. *Léon Bloy.*

. . . it is precisely at this point . . . where the poetic revolution crosses the revolution in the social and political and economic structure of the post-war world, which so deeply concerns our generation in this country . . . that the greatest victories of modern poetry may be won. *A. MacLeish.*

CHAPTER I

THE SIGNIFICANCE OF THE NEW POETRY

There are a good many reasons for reading contemporary poetry aside from the obvious one of getting aesthetic pleasure from it. Even if one gets no aesthetic pleasure from it, in the usual sense, it is worth reading. Even if one finds oneself poles apart from the attitudes and ethical standpoints of much of it, it is worth reading. For in it we have a disclosure of many profound and typical moods and trends of men today. The poets are apt to be the first to register the profound tides that move society and culture. They are the sensitive ones that first register and react to changes in the climate. They fish in deep waters and bring to light evidence from the inner world and the underworld by a kind of divination, evidence which we may well take into account. This is part of the mystery of the word. On the one hand there is the power of the word to create new worlds and destroy old, and the new poets are at it today as poets have always been. But there is the attendant and perhaps prior power of the word to get hold of yet obscure meanings and directions and values, and crystallize them. The new poets are doing that today. It is well expressed in the following lines of Geoffrey Scott:[1]

[1] An English poet, 1884-1929, whose mood identifies him with the poets we are considering. Our citations are from his scanty but precious poetic remains published, most of it for the first time, in 1931 (*Poems*, London, Oxford University Press).

Fishers of joy and pain
Grey words are we,
Who sift
Man's dream and drift;
Whose net
Under the moon is set
To drag the tidal secret of the world
Up from the shadowy sea . . .
                    "The Map of Spells"

The poets and artists of today are presenting us with the tidal secrets of the world, and these often illuminate the religious need and quest of our times. These strange voices, these protests, these maledictions, these despairs, proceed out of the Inferno of our age. When well heeded they bear witness to our contemporary maladies, doubts, remorses, prayers and illuminations. It will be evident that we are talking about the definitely *new* poets, the modernist poets, and not those who pursue today the old themes with the old outlook and the old forms.

The group we have in mind includes such different figures as T. S. Eliot, Ezra Pound, Robinson Jeffers, Eugene O'Neill, A. MacLeish, Conrad Aiken, Hart Crane, E. E. Cummings, D. H. Lawrence, W. H. Auden, Kenneth Patchen. They are alike only perhaps in their marked anti-traditionalism. Either in form or subject matter they sharply offend the lover of traditional poetry. Whether or not we find any beauty in their work, we will still find them significant for the light they throw on the times that produced them, on the world we live in today. They are indices of tensions that exist in our age. These are contemporaries of ours of special sensitiveness who are beset in a way many traditionalists are not, by the storms and stresses of the moral climate of today. When we take into the picture "modern" painting and "modern" music, do we not have evidence that there is a vast stratum of society today whose experience of life and whose outlook are greatly changed? This modernistic art is its indication. Berdyaev, the Russian Orthodox theologian, sees in futurist art, roughly parallel to all this, the evidence of the demoralization of Western culture. In any case, it is evidence of a change of culture for many. Some of it represents a criticism of modern life with which many of us would agree. Thus the protest of D. H. Lawrence against the machine age and machine age values is in order. The proletarian poets have opened wide areas of experience to our view. T. S. Eliot, of course, has moved in a definitely Christian direction, but even his earlier poetry, and in particular, *The Waste Land*, constituted a valid reaction against the barrenness of modern sophisticated life.

We can only understand and enjoy these new poets in proportion as we have shared their experiences. If we have felt the world and the age as they have we will not ask why they do thus and so—why they are preoccupied with suffering or disharmony or vice, why they are unorthodox in belief or ethical view, why they change the currency of poetic speech or the molds of poetic form. If we live at all sensitively or sympathetically in the life of today we cannot help welcoming the notes they strike at one point or another. We should naturally rejoice in their expression of the new sensibility that is ours as postwar occidentals. If we have not been artificially sheltered in these last decades we will share the tensions that afflict them, and we will find a corresponding release in their creative resolutions of these tensions.

This holds even for those of us who—unlike most of these poets—hold a positive religious faith of a Christian content and mood. Our Christian faith does not dissolve our solidarity with our age. The stresses and tensions of our age will take a different coloring for us as believers. We will deplore the despair or the error evident in many of these our fellows. We will often feel with tragic solicitude that we walk among them like Dante and Virgil in the lower rings of Hell.[2] But we should none the less often feel that their sense of the world is one we can understand. In fact, we should take it as a matter of grave concern if we find the new poets only sound and fury. If O'Neill or D. H. Lawrence or Robinson Jeffers or W. H. Auden or T. S. Eliot seem to speak in a totally different language than the one we know, we should ask ourselves if we have lived in our own time, genuinely. It is not enough to answer that the greatest poets are of all time. The world is going through so crucial a change at present that one may well be perturbed if he finds unintelligible the poets and arts that are expressing that change. We are not of course speaking of that contemporary work which is mainly pose or that proceeds to be different merely for reasons of experiment.

A chief reason for the failure of many to understand the new poetry, especially among religious people, is that

---

[2] "The unconcealed and palpable influence of the devil on an important part of contemporary literature is one of the significant phenomena of the history of our time." (Maritain, quoted by T. S. Eliot, *The Use of Poetry and the Use of Criticism*, p. 129.)

they have been closeted or blanketed from the forces of the world. It may be comparative economic security that disqualifies them or an insulated intellectual or social life. Such groups of people may have a wide range of sympathy and appreciation within their own world and will find much meaning in the traditional poetry and art which still continue to be produced, but they should not be surprised to find the art of their day a strange language. It was disturbing to hear a paper read some time ago by that year's recipient of our greatest honor in poetry—a paper that dealt satirically with the work of Ezra Pound and T. S. Eliot.[3] Aside from the legitimate fun which the speaker had with these men, we were left in doubt whether he had a full awareness of the levels of experience out of which they had done their best work.

The answer of the new poet to his critic is well brought out by a short poem of the same Geoffrey Scott mentioned above. He has in mind some well-known lines of W. H. Davies—lines in the approved Victorian tenor—which begin as follows:

> What is this life if, full of care,
> We have no time to stand and stare.
>
> No time to stand beneath the boughs
> And stare as long as sheep or cows . . .
> "Leisure."

Scott answers that the modern soul is too much haunted with profound bewilderments to be able to indulge such pastoral moods.

[3] R. Hillyer, *Some Roots of Poetry*, 1934.

I would my sight were formed to stare
In ecstasy on cows and trees,
To drink them in, and taste with care
Their sweet particularities;

And I would count them; but I go
Lost in a landscape of the mind,
A country where the lights are low
And where the ways are hard to find.

Such is the answer of the new man of our age for whom life's issues have become more drastic, and life's dimensions more extended.

So Archibald MacLeish testifies that the inner life is tyrannous and dark today. In his annotation of *Hamlet*,[4] Hamlet says to his mother,

I shall in all my best obey you . . .
                    Only
We have these dreams!
                    Only—
the old have announced us the
Irremediable woe, the ill
Long done, lost in the times before memory.

This sense of spiritual insecurity in modern poetry, while it prompts to negation, nevertheless has the merit of depth. These poets wrestle not against flesh and blood, but against principalities and powers, against the rulers of the darkness of the world. The modern world has become a haunted world. From an age of sunlight and clear outlines, an age of clear boundaries and patterns, when our

[4] *The Hamlet of A. MacLeish* (Boston, 1928), p. 5. On MacLeish, see appendix, p. 243.

friends and foes stood before us in unmistakable outline, we are passing into an age of twilight and phantoms. There is gain and loss in this. It is the passage from a secular to a spiritual outlook, at least to a more imaginative outlook. The phantoms, the principalities and powers have been there all the time, but they were pretty well fenced out by the nineteenth century with the exception of Poe and some French symbolists. The Victorian loved his ghost stories but his haunted house was usually on the edge of town or on the moors. Now the city itself is haunted. Even our religion has been until recently a well-ordered and well-rationalized one. The hatches have been well nailed down on the dynamics of the other world, and these have been able to make their incursions only in the unrecognized forms that modern psychology has demonstrated. Of late, however, there has been more commerce with them.

Feeling these things the modern has become impatient with the older poetry; impatient with rural sentiment, as in Scott's answer above, impatient with the fanciful tradition, impatient even with many more serious elements felt now as insufficiently real. And we get the turn toward the metaphysical and irrational. One reason why the Jesuit poet, G. M. Hopkins,[5] though a contemporary of the late Victorians, is claimed by the moderns, is that he had a sense of the fearful aspects of the mind, if not of society, which the modern feels:

> O the mind, mind has mountains; cliffs of fall
> Frightful, sheer, no-man-fathomed. Hold them cheap
> May who ne'er hung there. Nor does long our small
> Durance deal with that steep or deep . . .

[5] See appendix, p. 238.

Such examples show that the art of today in its own way often makes the same protest that recent theologians have been making in favor of a universe with dimensions and surprises. We must not conclude that nature is tamed, that the course of life is prophesiable, that the intellect can compass it. The human values we cherish are not enough. Man craves more. Only the other, the different, supernature, superman, can meet our need. Robinson Jeffers wants a deliverance from our human state. D. H. Lawrence would have us all "come through" from the puzzled and negative "mind" to a profound rebirth. There are religious implications of wide variety and significance in all this work.

The contrast in world view between new and old is well brought out by Geoffrey Scott in terms of the contrast of the lyre and the anvil as the proper symbol for the muse of poetry. His sonnet, "The Anvil, No. 1," finds the carol of life "Lean, disaccording, counter-crossed and jarred," and yet with something of exultation, none the less.

> Now come within, and hearken to my ringing:
> I am the Anvil: on my steely bed
> True dreams are gendered; I have other singing
> Than lyric air in lilted number led.
> My deeds are hopes split on the glitterless dark,
> My music is an iron starry shout,
> My suns are born to briefness like a spark:
> So was man's measure wrought and beaten out.
> Loud in my cave with grinding echoes rife,
> Lean, disaccording, counter-crossed and jarred,
> I mint the carol of created life,
> Chiming amiss with every cadence marred.
> If then, than these, more grateful tunes you crave,
> Choose to be deaf: your music's in the grave.

We will give attention below to the negation which characterizes so large a part of contemporary poetry and which
speaks in this poem. Fortunately this literature offers its
own evidence as to the sources of its world view, and far-
reaching insights can be gained from it as to the factors in
our age which make for disarray and despair. These factors
can often be seen at work in the personal history of the
poets themselves when it is known. Where these influences can be identified we have keys to the understanding
of widespread ravages in the moral and psychological life
of our time. It should be noted, however, that were we
inclined to apportion praise or blame to artists and writers
for their world view, attention should first be given to the
forces with which they have had to contend. A victory
over evil circumstance on a limited scale may yield a
lyric of affirmation, but it will hardly interest us as much
as a poem that registers the tragic view over against formidable adversaries. And the adversaries for sensitive men
in exposed places today are formidable. Those who retain
their optimism today are not always in exposed places—
exposed, that is, not only to the visible but also to the
invisible plagues of our time.

Among these contemporary poets and artists are those
that many are inclined to class as neurotic or even hysterical. This should not excuse us from considering them.
Men may be marked or hurt by experience—sensitive and
gifted men—and yet have much to communicate. It may
be because they have become the scapegoats and pioneers
of new ways of seeing, feeling and thinking, that they show
abnormalities. This latter factor is present in the case of
some of these poets. Their sensitiveness has led them to be

the first to feel the pressure of new conditions, and the resulting isolation has led in such natures to hurts and warpings and distortions. Many of the poets we list as on the border line of mental health have been there because they were the pioneers of mankind's advance into new capacities, new sensitivity, new awareness, in short, new consciousness: the Villons, Baudelaires, Poes, Dostoevskys. The complacency and inflexibility of the groups against which they rebelled have had much to do with their vagaries. More significant, however, for understanding artists of this type is the great word of Goethe: to seek is to err (*suchen is irren*). Men cannot leave the charted areas of human experience and pioneer out into the blank spaces that lie before the race without erring. Driven to new explorations of the soul and the heart, these seers find in part and err in part. They take the greatest hazards a man of thought and imagination can take, the hazards of sanity, and they know the cost of these explorations of the inner world. No wonder their work sometimes bears the marks of duress and may even appear tortured and hysterical. We have heard similar accents from Jeremiah.

CHAPTER II

THE MARKS OF THE NEW POETRY

It is evident that the terms "new" or "modern" or "modernist," even the term "experimental," applied to poetry and poets are very unsatisfactory. When one picks up an anthology of modern poetry one is as likely to find that it begins with Wordsworth or the Georgians as with Ezra Pound. The "new" poetry is less ambiguous but in poetry as in life hungry generations tread one another down, and D. H. Lawrence and Siegfried Sassoon are old, nay, the young English poet, C. Day Lewis, is consigned to an obsolete mediocrity by his peers of *New Verse*.[1] The term "experimental" appears to limit unduly the poets in view to those concerned with technique. All one can do is to

[1] On this group see appendix, p. 244. A good example both of the attitudes of the new poets to the traditional favorites and of the swift changes in the membership among the elect is found in the following comment by one of the *New Verse* editors on the apostasy of C. Day Lewis. The note is entitled, "Day Lewis Joins Up," referring to his joining the selection committee of the English Book Society. "On this Committee, Mr. Day Lewis no doubt will be Change, Revolution, Youth, the Rising Generation. But this ends his stance as the Poet writing thrillers . . . and establishes him as the Thriller Writer, the Underworld Man, the yesterday's newspaper, the grease in the sink-pipe of letters who has been posed for ten years as spring water. Think of Hardy, Yeats, Housman, Flecker, Pound, Lawrence, Eliot, Graves, Auden, Spender, Madge—could one have gone so treasonably against what is real? Mr. Day Lewis and his Legend are now liquidated: the liquid has flowed to its oily shape and low level in the old sardine tin of Respectability. Mr. Lewis has drained himself off, a Noyes, a Binyon, a Squire, a dullard. We can get along without him." *New Verse*, No. 35 (May, 1937), pp. 23, 24.

choose one of these terms and define it as best one may. After all when we speak of modern art or the new poetry today most will understand what is meant. It is the art or the poetry of the new epoch or period. Speaking as of 1925 on, say, it has not been difficult for us to recognize that a new climate of culture had begun for us after the war of 1914-1918 at least. Before that it was fitting to speak of Masefield or Noyes or Amy Lowell or Vachel Lindsay as the new poets or the modern poets. Not after that. It is true that on the Continent the new period came earlier and produced what we can call the precursive phases of the new poetry. In fact the new poetry has had its antecedents in England and America for some time. But the general recognition of the new epoch only came after the war, and with it a representative and authoritative group of new poets. Poets formed in the older period and surviving and productive in the new are most often not to be numbered among the new poets in the strict sense. Indeed, there are many young poets of today who have not felt the conditions of the new epoch and who write often able poetry for those who likewise have not felt these conditions or who for the time being set them aside.

The following "characteristics of modernity" are listed by Mr. Rodman in the Introduction to his *A New Anthology of Modern Poetry*.[2] He recognizes that "it may be difficult to dissociate some of them from the hallmarks of true poetry at any time."

. . . imagery patterned increasingly on everyday speech . . . absence of inversions, stilted apostrophes, conventional "poetic" language generally, except where used deliberately for in-

[2] New York, 1938.

cantatory effect . . . freedom from the ordinary logic of sequence, jumping from one image to the next *by association*
rather than by the usual cause-effect method . . . emphasis
on the ordinary, in reaction against the traditional poetic emphasis on the cosmic . . . concern with naked consciousness
and the newly identified "unconscious" as against "the soul"
. . . concern with the common man, almost to the exclusion
of the "hero" or extraordinary man . . . concern with the social order as against "heaven" and "nature."

John Crowe Ransom makes an attempt to distinguish
the "moderns" in his chapter, "Poets Without Laurels," in
The World's Body.[3] They are "those whom a small company of adept readers enjoys, perhaps enormously, but the
general public detests; those in whose hands poetry as a
living art has lost its public support. Consequently I do
not refer to such poets as Edna St. Vincent Millay and
Robert Frost, who are evidently influenced by modernism
without caring to 'go modern' in the sense of joining the
revolution . . . And still less do I refer to poets like E. A.
Robinson, Sturge Moore, and John Masefield, who are
even less modern." Mr. Ransom goes on to characterize
the modern poets as those who have failed "to identify
themselves with the public interests." They have refused
to carry on the time-honored role of public bard and
patriot, and especially have refused to be concerned with
moralities. In fact the specific character of the modern
poet is his insistence that aesthetics must be dissociated
from all else and sought with a single mind. He distinguishes two styles of modernity: the pure style, witness

[3] New York, 1938. Mr. Ransom, now teaching at Kenyon College in
Ohio, is one of the influential poets and intellectual leaders of the
"southern agrarian" group. See appendix, p. 247.

Wallace Stevens,[4] and the obscure style, witness Allen Tate.[5] The former avoids moralities by the choice of subject matter; the latter with more difficulty since he deals with significant materials, by reticence and obliquity of treatment. "Nevertheless, both types of poetry, obscure as well as pure, aim at poetic autonomy; that is, speaking roughly, at purity." At another point Mr. Ransom says, "Poets have had to become modern because the age is modern. Its modernism envelops them like a sea, or an air. Nothing in their thought can escape it." What he has in mind is the universal trend to specialization, which in the arts leads them to the autonomy or purity of which he has spoken.

Consideration of Mr. Ransom's view of the modern poet will show how elusive and difficult a category it is. In any case, he cannot be right (though we should note that Ransom apparently does not wholly approve of the type he describes). The irony of the situation is that one of the outstanding of the new poets, Mr. MacLeish, insists that the essential character of the new poet is that he represents a return to the role of public poet, using a public speech, concerned with moralities, practicalities, civics, competent to interpret the issues of everyday life. All this MacLeish sets in contrast to the introverted Victorian poet, the subjective dreamer, using a private speech, "special, formalized and poetized," and "suitable only to the private communication of certain special, formalized and

[4] A poet stemming from the imagist tradition, notable for distinction of manner and the abstract character of his subject matter. Mr. Stevens resides in Connecticut. His best known volume is *The Man With the Blue Guitar*, New York, 1937.

[5] See appendix, p. 248.

poetized emotions." "Public speech on the other hand is that human, living, natural and informalized speech, capable of the public communication of common experience, which, because it is capable of that use, cannot be confined to parlors or to proprieties or to those intimate whisperings in the personal ear which pass for purest poetry in the periods of decline."[6] That MacLeish is not solely speaking of poetry that enters the forum is evident from his praise of the language of T. S. Eliot, "taken from the mouths of his contemporaries," and from his praise of the later work of Yeats. For much of this is what we would have to call personal poetry of the inner life.

But MacLeish is particularly concerned that modern poetry should enter the forum, and his definition of it at its best requires that it should. For the results of the poetic revolution may prove to be most useful, he says, "at the point where the poetic revolution crosses the revolution in the social and political and economic structure of the postwar world." His own more recent work in this field is well known with the radio plays[7] and the verse in *Land of the Free*.[8] In an article in *Poetry*[9] recently MacLeish has attacked the group that calls for a "pure" poetry and has insisted on the call of poetry again to become "the one deliverer of the people." The divergence from Ransom's account of the new poetry is clear.

[6] "Public Speech and Private Speech in Poetry," *Yale Review*, Vol. XXVII, No. 3 (Spring, 1938), pp. 537, 538.

[7] *Panic: A Play in Verse* (Boston, 1935); *The Fall of the City: A Verse Play for Radio* (New York, 1937); *Air Raid: A Verse Play for Radio* (New York, 1938).

[8] New York, 1938.

[9] "In Challenge Not Defense," *Poetry, A Magazine of Verse*, Vol. LIi, No. iv (July, 1938).

Where Ransom has seen the criterion to be in aesthetic specialization and MacLeish in the use of a living public speech, Mr. Richard Schafer, in a brief rejoinder to the latter,[10] finds it in the concern with man as a social being. The poet of the last century was romantic: "the individual (not necessarily the poet himself) was the important thing in the world . . . Modern poetry is imbued with a communal spirit—not in the narrow doctrinal sense of economics or politics—but in the sense of all that men have in common and their interdependence." This notion of community of spirit is the dominant pattern of our time, says Mr. Schafer, and gives its stamp to contemporary poetry. This is evidently rather a correction than a rejection of MacLeish's view, carrying with it a vindication of some forms of what MacLeish would call "private speech."

Our conception of the modern poet will have to include both the pure poets of Ransom and such an exponent of public speech as MacLeish. Neither can exclude the other. They both belong to the new epoch. Neither are Victorians or Georgians. It is wrong to think that the ruling passion of the modernists is to separate aesthetics from moralities. Some like Wallace Stevens and Pound[11] and Tate appear to. Some like the later Yeats have implacable aesthetic demands but are incessantly at grips with moralities. Some like D. H. Lawrence and Jeffers are altogether more concerned with credo or protest than with aesthetics. What distinguishes them all as moderns is that they write as those who have lived since the flood—that is, since the World War and in general man's latter disillusioning dis-

[10] *Yale Review*, Vol. XXVIII, No. 4 (Summer, 1938).
[11] On this poet, see appendix, p. 240.

coveries of himself. Their act, as Ransom says in his Preface, "is not the act of a child, or of that eternal youth which is in some women,[12] but the act of an adult mind; and I will add, the act of a fallen mind, since ours too are fallen." "For such moderns as we are the poetry must be modern. It is not as in a state of innocence, to receive the fragrance of the roses on the world's first morning, that our moderns the scarred veterans may enact their poetry, but in the violence of return and regeneration."

This points us to the real answer. Berdyaev opens his great work, *Liberty and the Spirit*, with the following quotation from Léon Bloy: "Suffering passes, the fact of having suffered never passes." He then continues: "One must give this striking aphorism its fullest sense. One may surmount the experience of life, but the experience lived through remains forever part and parcel of the man and a modification, a widening, of his spiritual life. That which has been lived cannot be effaced . . . The man who has travelled widely through the worlds of the mind and spirit, who has been tested in the course of his quests and pilgrimages, will have a different spiritual growth from the sedentary individual to whom these worlds are unknown."

Berdyaev quotes this saying of Bloy apropos of the condition of the Russian Orthodox who have passed through the revolution as well as the intellectual struggles of the modern world, and for whom therefore the religious question must take a new form. But it applies equally, if in a different way, to the truly modern man of the West who has been subjected to the corresponding stresses of our times. His spiritual problems become different ones.

[12] Referring to a chapter in the book that deals with women poets.

His whole aesthetic, moral, cultural position will be different. He will want a new art and he will produce a new art. Not only his arts but his symbols and his dogmas will need to be transmuted. Abysses have been revealed to him in the discoveries and anarchies of the opening of the twentieth century. He has been scored by his experiences and can never know the world as it was known before. He has a new moral physiognomy, a new sensibility and if not a new soul he is in quest of one.

When we emphasize the difference between modern consciousness and the traditional we seem to be saying that only poets who write out of the former can truly interest us today. Mr. Ransom puts it this way. When we read the work of former ages we make "an adaptation of our minds to it" through our historical sense, and so are able to tolerate it. ". . . if we had begun to read a poetry of this old sort by saying, This was written last night by the poet around the corner, we could not have put up with it. If we throw away impatiently a contemporaneous poetry which displays archaisms of diction, what will we do with that which displays archaisms of temper? It looks spurious; for we require our art, and the living artists require it too, to be as contemporaneous as our banking or our locomotion."

Mr. Ransom disapproves of this procedure, but it represents that of many moderns toward traditional poetry. As a matter of fact they are wrong. There are many kinds of poetry and poetry has many kinds of appeal. Good poetry does not become obsolete just because it was not written out of the sensibility and mood of a new day. It may thereby lack a very important element of appeal. In cases where the issues of the contemporary outlook are pressing, all art alien to it may for the time being appear inconsequential, insipid, artificial. But our natures are too many-sided, our personalities are too comprehensive not to respond warmly to the thousand varied voices of man of all times.

A good opportunity to compare some of the features of old and new verse is afforded by two poems on a similar theme, one by Æ and one by Kenneth Patchen, the proletarian. The general theme is the contrast of the new and the old order. Let us see whether the pre-war, Celtic-romantic subject matter and style of Æ appears dated and whether his older form gives a sense of artificiality today.

Patchen's first poem in *Before the Brave*[13] reads as follows:

Turn out the lights around the statues.
Unlock the vaults of unhewn stone; put down
An order for new men. Place high the value
Of those others: do not forget what they have done.
Do not destroy. They built a world we could not use;
They planned a course that ended in disaster.
Their time is up. The curtain's down. We take power.
We're sorry they left so little. We wonder
If any will say of us: Do not forget. Do not destroy.
We wonder if they will mean it as much as we do now.
Turn out the lights around the statues.
What do you think the dead will wear next year?

To this we may add some lines from "Letter to the Old Men":

[13] New York, 1936. For detailed treatment of this poet see Chap. XV.

You stand on the ice of our hatred; your faces
Are turned to the wall. *You have not long.* . . .
        What have you left for us?
Our frontiers are all guarded; the day's work's begun.
The heroes flee your prisons; the sick approach the sun.
Our welcome is for others: your graves are ready, waiting
    . . . and pity
Can feed on the stone. For time and love
Are our ancestors, these, and these alone.

The staccato phrasings, the occasional strange tropes, give
a sense of deadly seriousness and hardness to this discourse.

ÆE writes "On Behalf of Some Irishmen Not Followers
of Tradition." It is one of his most magnificent poems and
must be given in full:

> They call us aliens, we are told,
> Because our wayward visions stray
> From that dim banner they unfold,
> The dreams of worn-out yesterday.
> The sum of all the past is theirs,
> The creeds, the deeds, the fame, the name,
> Whose death-created glory flares
> And dims the spark of living flame.
> They weave the necromancer's spell,
> And burst the graves where martyrs slept,
> Their ancient story to retell,
> Renewing tears the dead have wept.
> And they would have us join their dirge,
> This worship of an extinct fire
> In which they drift beyond the verge
> Where races all outworn expire.
> The worship of the dead is not
> A worship that our hearts allow,

Though every famous shade were wrought
With woven thorns above the brow.
We fling our answer back in scorn:
"We are less children of this clime
Than of some nation yet unborn
Or empire in the womb of time.
We hold the Ireland in the heart
More than the land our eyes have seen,
And love the goal for which we start
More than the tale of what has been."
The generations as they rise
May live the life men lived before,
Still hold the thought once held as wise,
Go in and out by the same door.
We leave the easy peace it brings:
The few we are shall still unite
In fealty to unseen kings
Or unimaginable light.
We would no Irish sign efface,
But yet our lips would gladlier hail
The firstborn of the Coming Race
Than the last splendour of the Gael.
No blazoned banner we unfold—
One charge alone we give to youth,
Against the sceptred myth to hold
The golden heresy of truth.

Here are some of the things that the modernist would
object to in this poem. The iambic tetrameter with its
Lady of the Lake movement and its tiresome rhymes:
clime, time; heart, start; youth, truth. The clichés: womb
of time, blazoned banner, Coming Race. The rhetorical
and artificial features: the capitalization of this last phrase
and the word "gladlier." The use of expressions that appear
to have great prestige for the imagination but which on

examination are found to be hopelessly vague: fealty to unseen kings, unimaginable light, golden heresy. These poems are full of dreams and visions and splendors. In sum, the total impression of the poem he would say takes one back to the sentiment of college fraternity sings or lodge love feasts where every eye is wet but no one believes a word of it. This is to say the worst that would be said about this poem by the modernist. It is not fair to it, but it shows through what spectacles many look today at traditional poetry. There has been so much spurious eloquence.

As to substance, the poems are written in different keys. Yet either writer conveys by impressive means the fact that two incommensurable orders of men confront each other. Æ hates his old order as much as Patchen does his. The one talks about the Coming Race and the unimaginable light and the other about new men and vaults of unhewn stone. There is no essential difference here. The modern radical pretends to scorn such idealism as that of the Irish romantic but he is almost as idealistic—which is to his credit. Yet Patchen deals with a conflict that affects the whole world and not just one people; a conflict that is contemporary; and he deals with it in unjaded terms. His manner and method bear the marks of the new poetry because his experience has stamped him with the new sensibility of our age.

CHAPTER III

THE TRADITIONALIST POET TODAY

We have referred to the particular tensions that have left their mark not only on recent poetry but on much recent art as a whole. For immense numbers of men these influences are decisive in the matter of spiritual values and outlook. On the basis of such experience men make what philosophy of life they can, but apart from exceptional cases, or apart from grace, if one puts it that way, it is not likely to be theist, let alone Jewish or Christian. Such handicaps to faith are real and tremendous. For the religionist they represent concrete challenges that must be dealt with. Our times face new conditions of living and thinking. The old balance of the spirit has been disturbed and we have to find a new one. While we may not view the facts of our day as these poets do, they can help us see what those facts, the elements of our spiritual problem, are.

It is quite true that many men today do not know these tensions or do not consent to the negations whether of thought or life which follow on them. We have here two different groups that we can distinguish. First, those that do not know these tensions. There are many men, artists and poets among them, that have not come between the upper and nether millstones of this generation. No sons or daughters of Adam go scot free from wear and tear and

heartache, but there are many privileged souls who have
been largely exempt and some of these are poets. They
have not been baptized with all the baptisms that our time
offers. They have not made the modern Anabasis or felt
loaded upon themselves the incubus of modern ill. They
were not there to

> Dare the unpastured dragon in his den,

whether in war, or in the morasses and jungles of peace,
and to carry his scars. They somehow fortunately escaped
the breath of the Black Plague of the times. Of these it
can be said that many are just simply fortunate, if it can
be called good fortune to be separated by their lot or by
innocence and naïveté from solidarity with the travail of
their fellows. For others harsher language is found by the
new poets. Sheltered by inherited securities both without
and within, aware of the throes at a distance, they have
been at least evasive, at worst traitorous. W. H. Auden
would include them with others pictured as follows:

> As it is, plenty;
> As it's admitted
> The children happy
> And the car, the car
> That goes so far
> And the wife devoted . . .
>
> Yes, and the success
> Let him bless, let him bless:
> Let him see in this
> The profits larger
> And the sins venal,

Lest he see as it is
The loss as major
And final, final.
On This Island, p. 32.

On the other hand, there are those, poets and artists included, who have known the tensions in some degree at least and who have refused to consent to the negations. We will defer to later chapters the discussion of those truly modernist poets who have come through a modernist negation and emerged with a positive outlook, still in the modernist temper. We are concerned here with traditionalist poets of today who have not been unaware of the time spirit but who have disregarded it or in any case not been shaped by it. It is not merely that they do not accept the negations. But their background and convictions have somehow obviated for them the characteristic note and mood of the new poets, not to mention their form.

Our attitude to these poets, the "traditionalists" of the older generation such as Bridges, Masefield, Noyes, Davies, de la Mare, and the younger group sharing their outlook, is a difficult one especially if we hold traditional religious convictions. From that point of view these people and many more are on the side of the angels. We do not have to suspend any disbelief in reading them. They write out of a fund of attitudes, valuations and responses that we share with them. We count it of major importance that there should be these men to exalt the things most worthy of poetry: love, responsibility, confidence, the transfiguration of life. We know that much of their work is not to be counted great poetry. We know that it does not echo many of the stresses of the time. But in it is evidence of experience mastered, and triumphed over: the individual's everyday human lot surmounted by courage and faith, and even the greater enigmas resolved if only by echo and by proxy.

But for all the quality of these poets we miss in them the marks of what has become essential for us. We know they have wrestled with their day in various ways, but somehow their work has not the signature which some of us seek. Have they "been there"? We are not sure. It is evident that they have emerged triumphant. But over what? Over how much? For our part, it seems to us that we met with Leviathan in the thickets of Villers-Cotterets in 1918. Many of us are of those that have

> sat by Thebes below the wall
> And walked among the lowest of the dead.[1]

Have *they* met with Leviathan? Have they been through the lava and the lifeless air that many moderns report? Have they

> heard the key
> Turn in the door once and turn once only
> . . . each in his prison
> Thinking of the key?[2]

Have the idealist poets been there? We are not sure.[3] We appraise their work as poetry apart from all else and enjoy

---

[1] *The Waste Land,* lines 245, 246.
[2] *Ibid.,* lines 411-414.
[3] See Allen Tate's poem, "The Romantic Traditionalists":
> They never saw the dark
> Rigid, they never knew alarm . . .
>   *The Mediterranean and Other Poems,* p. 23.

what is excellent. With a backward look, for the moment forgetting our new necessities, we enjoy what we once saw and loved. We recognize insights and beauties that because we are believers we glory in. But beyond that we miss much.

MacLeish, in his paper on Public Speech and Private Speech, can say of the traditionalist poets writing today: "the poets of our time to whom the revolution in poetry was unreal, or who were unable for one reason or another to profit by it, have found themselves face to face with a brutal choice—to resign either from their age or from their art. Many of them, unable to comprehend within a rhetorical art a generation of violence and tragedy and menace, have been driven either out of their art into silence or out of their age into dreams."

D. H. Lawrence makes a dry comment on one of the Georgian poets who was afraid to be seen with him. "When I lunched with —— he says, 'Isn't it remarkable, how the poets are returning to Beauty!'—he was afraid to walk with me up the Mall afterwards, and ran away like a respectable rabbit. What I want to know is, was it my appearance, or my reputation, or his? *Bel Dio!*"

These poets in their turn can make a telling answer. One of them writes in a personal letter: "But granted the defects of impatience in me, I still think that too often the *good radical* modern poets are overlooked for the *bad radical* ones. Frost is far more radical in form than Jeffers . . . E. A. Robinson is more modern than D. H. Lawrence in his ideas. And Conrad Aiken and T. S. Eliot are far less radical poets than Lindsay and Sandburg. It all depends on what you mean by *New Poetry* . . . Frost is a sensible radical and a sincere one; ——— is a cheap jack false one. He matches indigestion for a philosophy."

The present writer has heard a very cogent and vigorous scolding applied to certain of the modernist poets by another writer, R. P. T. Coffin. He knows the age of Chaucer and he points out facts that are discomforting to the argument of our foregoing chapters. It is there insisted that our age is a hard age in which to maintain faith. Look at the fourteenth century, says Mr. Coffin. The Hundred Years' War that devastated Europe; the Black Death that swept in three successive waves over the Western world and slew from one-third to one-half the population; the disintegration of spiritual and moral authority as represented especially in the church; the world was so terrified by these visitations that men were driven to frenzy and the end of the world imminently expected. And yet Chaucer managed to retain his sanity and humor, to master his experience and to write in the vein we know. The whole point of the matter is courage. These new poets, these modernists, are defeatists! Thus the debate is engaged.[4] One will find further illustrations from this side in J. C. Squire's *Tricks of the Trade* and in the volume, *A Letter to Robert Frost and Others* by Mr. Robert Hillyer.

The fact is that men's areas of experience are very dissimilar. This is a pluralistic world; there is room for many kinds of poetry. Nor can any man say what or how much

---

[4] A skeptical reader of recent poetry writes to the author as follows: "I think the new insulin treatment for schizophreniacs could be used with our poets. Dose them till their temperature rises to the danger point, then let them down with a bang and in the jar a poem would be born . . . The whole study of schizophrenia is interesting to the student of modern poetry. One patient says, 'I cannot carry on a conversation without having other sentences get in between.'"

another man has had to endure or overcome. In any case, Mr. Robert Hillyer's world of experience, which included the war, and no doubt the new psychology and some awareness of social anarchy, nevertheless is poles apart from the world experienced by many other artists of today. He has his audience of those that see the world as he does. The new poets have their audience of those that see the world as they do. The world will slowly pass its judgment on both. "Every man's work shall be made manifest . . . and the fire shall try every man's work of what sort it is." There will be many surprises on both sides at the verdicts of posterity. For both sides build, if partially, upon truth, and wisdom is justified of its children. If we can imagine a Day of Judgment for poets, a sort of heavenly *Jeux Floraux*, we may well imagine the children of sweetness and light astonished at the awards made to those they had thought were the sons of Belial. Behold the Baudelaires, the Villons, the blasphemers and the deniers, receiving the palm for the virtues of "love and awareness": "these are the primary, essential values" (Aldous Huxley). But contrariwise, behold the scorned Victorian poets crowned with wreaths, together with Bridges, Abercrombie, and Frost, concerning whom the Judge shall say to the realists: "these other sheep also I have which are not of your fold." But we suspect that the Judge will be partial to the publicans and sinners.

We have spoken of the injustice done to the new poets by the "old," and our special concern here has been to vindicate the new. These labor under the handicap that a greater Rebel referred to: "No man also having drunk old wine straightway desireth new; for he saith, the old is better." But there is one common charge made against the traditional poets of far-reaching character which calls here for attention, the charge of escapism. The charge touches not only the poet but the religionist. It is made against the poet who abstains from social themes, the poet of "private speech" rather than "public speech," or more generally against those that pretend to use poetry as a form of disciplined contemplation.

The situation here corresponds exactly to that in the field of religion. If the exercises of the inner life and the celebration of personal experience are "escape" in one they are in the other. If they are diversions from objectivity and social realism in one they are in the other. What makes the charge difficult to refute is the partial guilt of both religionists and poets. There are poets who make of poetry a sentimental religion, whose practice they take as excusing them from the common demands of life. There are those whose poetry is a persistent excitation of their deeper emotional life of a purely subjective character. There are those who as we shall see in connection with the discussion of Hart Crane, relate this Narcissism to the outer world, not with a true objectivity, but as a form of self-aggrandizement, the object being sensation, not knowledge. Religious mysticism and sentiment have their corresponding vices.

But a sharp distinction must be made between all such selfish forms of romantic poetry and legitimate "private speech" or lyricism or introspection. The charge that forms of *high* religion are an opiate is a precise contradiction of its character and shows elementary ignorance of the history of religion. Similarly, the charge of escapism

against traditional and idealist poetry is an absurd confusion of facts, and betrays a naïve and simplistic conception of human action. Even the man who prides himself on his forthright action or concern with the world of
men has his mysticism, his prayer, his worship. His will
to action has been fed on imagination and his motives
have become urgent through contemplation. The form
his action takes has a relief not to say crudeness which he
takes to be the only kind of action, and he therefore fails
to recognize action in subtle and perhaps more potent
form.

Those who have overheard Robert Frost talking to himself, with somewhat more than the usual number of asides
and parentheses, on this subject of escapism will not
soon forget it. Undoubtedly he has been nettled by the
continual cropping up of this topic as concerns his poetry
and that of his friends in Amherst and Maine.

"As though a man who likes to live in the country is
disqualified! As though a person had to live in New York
to be a poet! Religion, escape! These themes of mine,
escape!

"No. My life has been the pursuit of a pursuit. Not a
retreat. Near the beginning of Bunyan's book Pilgrim
says, 'I think I see it,' and the rest of the book is the
search. Escape may be the opposite: attack. Every man's
life is a *wreaking* of himself upon something or someone.
His base of operations is a personal matter. The only
thing, the big thing, for us all is attack, finding something
we have to take by the throat.

"If you draw back far enough to strike a blow they
say 'escape.' (A poem must have a point like a joke, point

and thrust.) If you draw off it's because you have a longer spear, perhaps. (It's like a boy and the running broad jump.) My weapon's a lance and I have to back up to use it right. The dirk is a city weapon . . ."

Undoubtedly Mr. Frost and Mr. Hillyer like Æ and Tagore *are* concerned with the human values they see about them and act in accordance with their gifts and vocation. They too have their avenues of social action. But we should not lose from sight in stressing this that between the agnostic or cynical modernist and the poet who still believes in God and man there will always remain a deep distinction. The latter will make no apologies for his private poetry because he knows the reality and fruitage of his inner world, which is yet not inner but the real world. In like manner Berdyaev deals with the hostility of the Marxists, Nietzsche and others to Christianity. He recognizes that there has been a perversion of Christianity by Christians "in the fact that Christianity was understood solely as a religion of individual salvation . . . But there will always remain a deep distinction between those who believe in the existence of a supreme spiritual world, in the attachment of man to the eternal life in God, and those who believe only in the world, in its self-sufficiency, in earthly joy, as the end of life. . . . Christianity has a social side; in it there must be revealed the truth regarding just and brotherly construction of human society; but it is primarily and always will remain a mystical and spiritual religion."[5] The same affirmation is made in non-religious terms by Mary M.

[5] "Grounds for Hostility to Christianity," *The Student World*, Vol. XXXI, No. 2 (Second Quarter, 1938), pp. 111-112.

Colum in concluding her volume of literary criticism, *From These Roots:* "Yet just as surely as time is composed of night and day, life is composed of dream and external reality, and the advancement and happiness of man depend not only on the elevation of his everyday life, but on the elevation of his dream-life."

The disqualification of affirmative religious poetry as "escape" arises then out of a confusion of two different kinds of mysticism. There is a healthy kind of mysticism that nourishes and there is an unhealthy kind that destroys. Either kind constitutes a withdrawal from the world, either kind can result in first-class poetry, but only the latter can properly be called "escape." It alone is truly egotistical, willful and unreal. Traditionalist poetry is not to be scorned solely on the ground of subjectivism and introspection. This remains one of the supreme areas of poetic creation.

CHAPTER IV

THE PROBLEM OF RELIGIOUS POETRY IN AMERICA

The status of the traditionalist poet today is often further complicated by another fact. Strangely enough, despite Virgil, Dante, and Milton, and in our times Claudel, Tagore and Rilke, there is in the minds of some a question whether religion is a proper subject matter for poetry. Just as there is a question whether another ardently espoused theme of salvation, namely, communism, is a proper subject matter for poetry. The celebration of religious sentiment in poetry troubles the critic. It adds to the complexity of the matter. Such poets are deprecated. If their talent is indubitable they are gotten around by being placed in a special category: "a Catholic poet," or, a Celtic mystic with a perverse and obscurantist Way; or, worst of all, a pietist. It is true that if the religious quest is sufficiently animistic, especially totemistic; if the Golden Bough makes its presence felt; if Jesus and Judas are made to change roles, and a sadistic ethics are discernible, then the ban on religious poetry is strangely lifted, and such poets are counted as not muddying their aesthetics by didacticism. Now there is a reason for these forms of primitivism and the orthodox are much to blame, but clearer thinking about the rights of religious poetry of any kind are in order.

We may simplify the question by granting that a great quantity of very ordinary religious verse is written by believers of all persuasions—especially in hymns: we may safely say that modern hymns are a form of occasional verse; the same is true of the poetry in religious periodicals. Such expressions of piety, even when competent and written with some chastity of sentiment, have an adventitious advantage with believers that tends to obscure their limitations. What adult evangelical is able to judge dispassionately the hymns on which he was brought up? The critics then have just as much right to ignore religious verse as any other kind of *verse*. Be it said, however, that a much stronger case can be made out than is usually realized for popular verse of commonplace character. Now and then even the artists "discover" some corner of popular lore and literature. Negro spirituals had to wait to have their merit recognized. Carl Sandburg has canonized another area of unliterary discourse in *The People, Yes*. We prophesy that some literary anthropologist will some day discover the humble hymn book. Again, even where the material is execrable as art it may serve as a carrier of unlimited associations and have a great value as symbol. This is true whether of Catholic images, of evangelical hymns or of patriotic anthems.

The problem is part of a larger problem which has been much discussed lately, the problem of art and propaganda. Without raising that whole question anew, we venture the following statements, bearing in mind Eliot's discussions.[1] Poetry of value will not be written except out of some set

[1] Papers on "Experiment in Criticism" and "Poetry and Propaganda" in Zabel, *Literary Opinion in America*, pp. 11 ff. Also, the study of Dante in *Selected Essays*.

of living interests of the writer. There is hardly any such thing as a poetry that makes no confession at all. The art for art's sake of the nineteenth century proposed itself really as a form of, or substitute for, religion. Critical theory in the seventeenth and eighteenth centuries in France and England viewed poetry, indeed, as a fine art, "a means of refined and intellectual pleasure." As such it was kept clear of much with which today it overlaps. But we have only to think of Milton, Racine, Pope to see how poetry, however mindful of its artistic canons, has taken in ethical ground. It is true that poetry that is honestly dramatic, either in the sense of Shakespeare's plays or in the sense that the writer detaches himself from his poem, will give no direct confession of the poet. Both because he was a dramatic poet and because his attitudes had the universality and reticence of nature itself, Shakespeare does not impose his view of life upon us. "Shakespeare does certainly influence us; but as he influences each man according to his own education, temperament and sensibility, and as we have no clue to the relation of his influence upon any one mind with what Shakespeare actually meant, it is almost fantastic to call it propaganda." Eliot then would place Shakespeare at one pole of a series and a poet like Dante at the other. Goethe would come in between somewhere. All poets can be placed according as they have a completely dominating and confessed set of beliefs, or only a sporadic dependence on special convictions. The reader will have to make the best of those beliefs to which he is antagonistic by suspending his disbelief and by understanding them as best he can. Above all he will try to judge the poetry as poetry whether he agrees with it or not. While "the 'greatness' of literature cannot be determined solely by literary standards we must remember that whether it is literature or not can be determined only by literary standards."

On such grounds an impartial reader of poetry should be prepared to welcome poetry written from religious convictions provided that it be poetry. It will probably remain true that he will be disqualified from a full appreciation of poetry written out of convictions that he does not share. Yet a Christian believer can deeply enjoy the *Rubáiyát*, as indeed he enjoys the book of Ecclesiastes, and there would seem to be no reason why a well-disposed agnostic should not deeply enjoy Dante.

The rub today seems to come with religious poetry that has an ethical or idealist, not to say didactic, element in it. We have in mind poems like Alfred Noyes' *Watchers of the Sky*, William Vaughn Moody's "The Fire Bringer," Abercrombie's "The Sale of St. Thomas," Ralph Hodgson's "The Song of Honour," Masefield's "The Everlasting Mercy" and Ridgely Torrence's "Eye-Witness." A great deal of the competent poetry written and read in Anglo-Saxon countries belongs in this area. In the immediate past we think of Kipling and of Edwin Markham. This kind of poetry suggests a number of questions. Why is it not better on the whole? What hopes are there for that deeper passion that can make such quasi-religious poetry more significant? Is there not some relation between the weakness of this kind of traditional poetry and contemporary religious life itself? On the other hand, are contemporary critics fair to such work? For note that they give at least a grudging hearing to Catholic and Anglo-Catholic poets and artists, or to various forms of esoteric mysticism or even primitivism. Does no poetry in the Puritan tradition, the tradition of Milton, achieve marked literary excellence today? Did the Reformation deprive its followers of an adequate symbolism for works of the imagination? Or is it that the modern world has a bad conscience or a repression that manifests itself in an inflamed soreness wherever the ethical strain in Christianity is emphatic?

It is true that most of this poetry does not conform to our demands of modernist poetry. Its affirmation is not that of men who have written around and about the particular maladies of our period. But the prevailing attitude of criticism to this kind of poetry is such as to make us doubt whether it is unprejudiced toward religious poetry, and whether, if a first-rate poet of the Puritan tradition appeared they would value him truly.

Milton was a Protestant poet who is still highly ranked but he is a special case. For one thing he is a major poet and for another he was first a professional poet in the worldly sense. Indeed, he may be the exception that proves the rule, if we accept the view of one critic: "Milton is . . . a grand pagan, and half knows it."

But apart from any predisposition of the critics, a very significant query is forced upon us. Are we not pointed toward the conclusion that no really sustained first-class poetry is possible in the Puritan tradition? Has Protestantism any living body of symbolism such as Catholicism has that may serve the artist? Certainly the wealth of Biblical imaginative material that Milton and Bunyan used has lost the relevance and prestige that it once had with the poet's reading public. The Negro spirituals alone today make a successful appeal to it. Masefield's "The Everlasting Mercy," Vachel Lindsay's "General Booth" and Kipling's work could still do so twenty years ago but the time is rapidly passing when this is still possible. Religious poetry from poets of that tradition is likely to take a pagan direction as in Miss Millay's "Renascence." In general may we not say about the Puritan tradition in our time that not only has its Biblical foundation lost its hold with the public as a resource for literature, but that this is only one aspect of the decline of the tradition itself. Hawthorne, indeed, was the last important figure to write out of an American culture still powerfully unified and animated by Puritanism. Already when Emily Dickinson wrote, as Tate has shown, that day was passing. Emerson's outlook testifies to the new independence and individualism, and at the same time to the new America which in industrialism and in free thought had exchanged its older religious vitality for a spiritual disorganization that has come down to the present day in successive phases. The Puritan inheritance is indeed ineradicably in the stock, and its stamp on the nation will never be removed. But it has been deeply overlaid by new influences, and today it does not offer any easy resource for an imaginative creation.

We shall discuss at another point the significant fact that when T. S. Eliot, of New England descent and New England temper, reached beyond his contemporary dilemmas to triumphant affirmation, he had to pass beyond the New England tradition to do so. E. A. Robinson, who fought the issue out in the framework of his forefathers could not go beyond an heroic stoicism.

These limitations of contemporary American life for

literature of deep religious import are discussed by contemporary criticism. The following somewhat parenthetical remarks in an essay on Hart Crane by Allen Tate are revealing.[2] "The American mind was formed by the eighteenth-century Enlightenment, which broke down the European truths, and gave us a temper deeply hostile to the making of new religious truths of our own." And later: "The age is scientific and pseudo-scientific, and our philosophy is John Dewey's instrumentalism. And it is possibly this circumstance that has driven the religious attitude into a corner where it lacks the right instruments for its defense and growth, and where it is in a vast muddle about just what these instruments are." These considerations are adduced to explain the inability of Hart Crane to create a successful myth in *The Bridge*.[3] The statement concerning the role of the Enlightenment is interesting as showing what Mr. Tate and many others apparently hold about America: namely that the Puritan imprint was not an indelible one and is not still the ultimately determining one. Mr. Siegfried as a visiting observer was sure that the contrary was the case.[4] And Howard Mumford Jones at the Harvard Tercentenary Symposium made an emphatic correction in the current view of the eighteenth century. "A saltatory conception of American literature, with . . . its picture of a libertarian ideology opportunely arriving from Europe to free the American mind from its theological prison-house like the angel liberating Paul and Silas—this it is which has produced the confusions I have sketched." "The story of

[2] *Reactionary Essays*, pp. 34, 35.
[3] See below, pp. 122 ff.
[4] André Siegfried, *America Comes of Age* (New York, 1927).

eighteenth-century American development is the story of the slow fusion of a culture founded in Protestant dissent with certain of the secular ideas of classicism . . . the result was, on the whole, a secular, but not a skeptical, victory—that is to say, the transfer of the problem of universal order from the theological to the moral sphere." "I suggest that the central problem in American thought, at least until late in the nineteenth century, is the problem of the moral order of the universe—a problem so primary as on the whole to subordinate almost all other philosophical and aesthetic considerations to this central question."[5]

Both Mr. Tate and Mr. Jones would probably agree that *at present* the American scene is too secularized and disintegrated to offer the poet the means of a large-scale construction in a Puritan or even a Christian frame of reference. But Mr. Jones alone seems to recognize that it is in this direction that we must look for any hope of a successful body of myth or imaginative symbol. The point is that American reactions are fundamentally dominated still by Puritan religious and ethical motives, and a secularized or neo-Catholic criticism is out of key with it and unable to do full justice to its trends. Thus the typical modern critic, "formed by the eighteenth century enlightenment" and "in a vast muddle about the religious attitude" is unlikely to appreciate fully the work stemming from the Puritan tradition. Too great an effort of suspension of disbelief is necessary. This is an important factor in the insufficient recognition given to some of the older poets like Browning. More recent poets in this tradi-

[5] The Drift to Liberalism in the American Eighteenth Century, in *Authority and the Individual* (Cambridge, 1937), pp. 332, 333, 336.

tion suffer similarly. The high value put by the new critics on many writers is unconsciously due to an agreement in world view and vice versa.

Yet it must be admitted that traditionalist poets writing out of this inheritance do not satisfy our contemporary needs. They do not explore that inheritance deeply enough to tap springs of unmistakable power. They do not relate that inheritance to the modern mood and its ills. But in both respects they resemble most of the churches of the Protestant tradition. We will have greater religious poetry when the devout and mystical poets among us enter as deeply into the experience of grace as our poets of nega-tion enter into the experience of perdition. Seizures in a vernal wood, didactic outbursts about bombing planes, and dilute personal lyricism will not cope with the works of the devil as they are exhibited to us by the twentieth century. We are told by Jeremiah that the prophet's word is "like as a fire, and like a hammer that breaketh the rock in pieces." We have to take this largely on faith as far as our generation is concerned. The emergence of poets adequate to deal with the issues of our world crisis in terms of faith requires first the chastening and deepening all along the line of American religious life. Some of the world-shaping conviction of the Reformation must be re-captured and some of its apocalyptic ardor. Those old springs that fed the modern world have been buried deep in the sands and need to be uncovered. It is not a matter of a new revivalism on the pattern of the eighteenth and early nineteenth centuries. It is a matter rather of a new liberation in continuation of the Reformation, carried out this time not against a medieval church but against a modern neopaganism, a neopaganism found not only in the ideologies of apostate states but also in the very air we breathe in the democratic nations. The discrimination and power for such tasks, whether on the part of prophet, reformer or poet, depend on renewal of the Christian tradition in our time. That the tradition can renew itself is already demonstrated at those points where the irrepressible conflict with neopaganism has already begun, that is, in the totalitarian states. The consequent tragedy brings both understanding and utterance.

Even when poetry of religious or ethical content lacks of supreme achievement, however, modern literary criticism should be prepared to give it its due. At the root of the whole issue of the place of religious poetry is the valuation placed upon the classical tradition. As long as the Hebrew tradition is excluded as "sacred" we will have no balanced view of the scope of literature. It cannot be insisted often enough that Western culture has two roots, a Greek and a Hebrew. But professional criticism has tended with few exceptions to ignore the Hebrew models and norms. Ezra Pound and the imagists have compassed heaven and earth to find new fertilizing factors for English poetry: in Chinese and Japanese literature, in Anglo-Saxon, in Sanskrit, in Provençal, in Persian. But no signs of attention to Hebrew poetry and prophecy![6] There never

---

[6] Mr. Pound has recently given vent to his profound antipathy for the Old Testament scriptures, and not the Old Testament only. "If anyone in calm mind will compare the Four Classics (of Confucius) with the greatly publicized Hebrew scriptures he will find that the former are a record of civilized men, the latter the annals of a servile and nomadic tribe that had not evolved into agricultural order. It is with the greatest and most tortuous difficulty that the Sunday School has got a moral teaching out of these sordid accounts of lechery, trickery and isolated

was a more striking example of straining out the gnat and swallowing the camel. When modern critics make any reference to the Bible, they appear to know that they are walking on unsafe ground. To them Jeremiah is nothing but a "weeping prophet"; Amos and Isaiah are examples of embittered enviers of human joy. The reviewers of Thomas Mann's *Joseph and His Brothers* are hard put to it to make an impression of being oriented.

Those who are familiar with the rhythmic prophecy of Israel at its greatest in Jeremiah and the second Isaiah; those who know Job and the Psalms as poetry; those who know the peculiar values of Hebrew epic in contrast to Homer and Virgil; such will never consent to let their norms for literature be determined by Hellenic and Renaissance patterns. With such a background no modern or contemporary literature is immediately to be deprecated because it has "didactic" content. It must, indeed, pass the test of literature. But other things being equal, that literature which concerns itself with the greater subject

---

acts of courage, very fine and such as could be paralleled in the annals of Mohawks and Iroquois . . . Jehovah is a semitic cuckoo's egg laid in the European nest. He has no connection with Dante's god. That later concept of supreme Love and Intelligence is certainly not derived from the Old Testament." ("Mang Tsze," *The Criterion*, July, 1938, pp. 617, 618.) In Mr. Pound's view the trouble with those that gave us the Bible was that they were not "civilized." What he wants first, along with Confucius and Mencius, is bread and amenities. With these disorder will cease, for men will then live organically and in accordance with nature. One hardly knows where Mr. Pound is most astray: in his ignorance of Old Testament backgrounds, in his view of the sources of medieval theology, or in his naïve optimism with regard to human nature. The fact is that his admiration for Dante places him in an awkward position. For Dante receives his basic criteria of God and of human existence from the Bible. Pound must therefore either value the Bible or deny its significance for Dante. He chooses the latter alternative and throws himself into the camp of Rosenberg and the Fascists generally.

matter, such as "the moral order of the universe," will be the greater literature; and for the American folk tradition, that literature that shows a mastery of the raw material of life in terms of religious insight will strike most deeply into the heart of the times.

PART TWO. FACTORS MAKING FOR NEGATION

Shakespearean fish swam the sea, far away from land;
Romantic fish swam in nets coming to the hand;
What are all those fish that lie gasping on the strand?
W. B. Yeats, "Three Movements."

"nè morte il giunse ancor, nè colpa il mena,"
respose il mio maestro, "a tormentarlo;
ma par dar lui esperienza piena,

a me, che morto son, convien menarlo
per lo inferno quaggiù di giro in giro . . ."[1]
Inferno 28:46-50

---

[1] "Neither has death come to him as yet, answered my master, nor does guilt bring him here to torment him; but to give him full experience, I who am dead must needs lead him down here through Hell from circle to circle."

CHAPTER V

NEW VIEWS OF THE SELF

The understanding of modernistic art and poetry is greatly aided by some knowledge of the aims of the artists. Whether apparent formlessness or recurrent notes of the ugly or the discordant, such are usually deliberate and have their reasons. The conception of what art is, and what it is for, changes or returns to older norms, and the observer should be prepared to revise his views as to these matters.

Poetry in its greatest interpreters has been looked on as having an aim beyond that which "the plain reader" often assigns it. He often asks that poetry shall deal with the bright side of life; he is inclined to identify it with that which is "inspiring"; he lays emphasis on qualities pleasing to eye and ear: the verbal music of its lines or the pictures it evokes. He is concerned often with craftsmanship, not in the great sense of style but in the sense of the jewel cutter. But the great critics from Aristotle on have looked on poetry as concerned with truth, as testifying to reality, as at least re-presenting, if not interpreting, the world. By comparison with this, matters of lyrical pleasure or picture-language are minor. Many of the new poets are concerned with the nature of life—those aspects which the imagination can capture better than the understanding, be they beneficent or destructive, fair or ugly. This is not to say that they are indifferent to "form."

Those who think of art idealistically, therefore, as the language of the soul[1] and the embodiment of Beauty are unprepared for the new work, and, indeed, for much of the old. The recent school of poets gives us a poetry of conflict rather than of fruition. Poetry is not the treatment of joy and triumph only. Conflict and despair are likewise important subject matter. The poet who refracts these tellingly through his own mind is reporting on life significantly. Whether he has dominated his area of experience triumphantly or not is a further issue.

No doubt the real greatness of poetry is in proportion to the ability of the artist to dominate great fields of conflict and experience. Even in the matter of form such mastery of life is important. Mr. Yvor Winters has made it his special emphasis to point out that imperfection and unintelligibility are closely related to personal inadequacy in face of the given experience. He uses the term "moral" in discussion of these matters in a somewhat special sense. But may we not accept his conclusion, both as to substance and to form: "If a poem, in so far as it is good, represents the comprehension on a moral plane of a given experience, it is only fair to add that some experiences offer very slight difficulties and some very great, and that the poem will be the most valuable, which, granted it achieves formal perfection, represents the most difficult victory. In the great tragic poets, such as Racine or Shakespeare, one feels that a victory has been won over life itself, so much is implicated in the subject matter."[2]

---

[1] Mr. Ransom quotes with some satisfaction a rebuke of Tennyson by George Moore to the effect that "the Victorian could never reconcile himself to finishing a poem without speaking about the soul."

[2] *Primitivism and Decadence, A Study of American Experimental Poetry* (New York, 1937). On Winters, see appendix, p. 249.

We may then recognize that the supreme uses of poetry are with reference to themes of fruition, solution, victory, but in the most immediate relation to effort and conflict. But so rare is such poetry that we may well choose an authentic poem of defeatism over a secondhand poem of faith. Truth is so important that the cry of bitterness or the notation of despair may make far more important art than the sincerities often borrowed or forced of the "right-thinking."

A poet should be thought of as a person more than commonly aware, vibrating and responding to the world and bearing witness to it, but one necessarily who has the gift of the artist in bearing witness that has form: that is a saliency, a relief, an immanent energy which adequately correspond to the dynamic character of experience itself. That is the essence of the matter of form: it is the imprint and signature of power. The crystal mutely testifies to enormous energies. The poem that has character, that is, imprint, testifies to a high order not necessarily of emotional but at least of psychical energies. For the *kind* of form we may expect of an artist great latitude must be allowed. There are many kinds of crystals in the earth. Regularly rhymed and rhythmic verse is only one family in the many forms of poetry. As we recall the unlimited varieties of experience that come to men, changing with race and decade, we will anticipate wide departures in the types of art that they will occasion.

The poet responds, then, to the world. And since the world is a profound and bewildering and grandiose affair, we ought not to be satisfied with any report of that world in art which does not bear witness to its tragedy and its magnificence. It is one of the merits of modern poetry that it at least bears witness to the dimensions of life, if only in negative terms. It has the sense of the "abyss." What Glenway Wescott left America for ("Goodbye, Wisconsin"[3]) and found in Paris, a culture that "has death in mind," that is, one that measures and savors life over against the thought of mortality—that is found in this poetry. It sees the dizzy precipices of the soul; it sees the latent anarchies of the tribe. Here we have what is needed for true poetry and more possibilities than for some time of great poetry. "The essential advantage for a poet is not to have a beautiful world with which to deal: it is to be able to see beneath both beauty and ugliness; to see the boredom, and the horror, and the glory." (Eliot)

The following characterization of the negative temper of the modernist poets is given us by Riding and Graves in *A Survey of Modern Poetry*. This whole section in Chapter IX should be read, especially for its clarification on the note of irony in these poets. The present passage in some ways betrays the date (1929) at which the book was published. "The present lost generation does not feel its lack of ideals as sinfulness, but rather as sophistication. It does not love itself, but it does not hate itself. It does not think much of life, but neither does it think much of death. It is a cynically common-sense generation which would not, for example, consider dying for the freedom of a small enslaved nation or for literary fame, for that matter . . . Because it emphasizes the wit in common-sense rather than the common-sense in wit, and because wit is cynical, it is a cynical generation; yet not a sentimental

[3] The collection of short stories with this title (New York, 1928) is introduced by an essay with the theme above stated.

generation, because of its common-sense; nor a pessimistic generation, because pessimism is sentimental."[4] We would query the statement that our generation does not think much of death. The passage means, in view of the paral-lelism, that it does not value either life or death highly; but the further sense is involved: it does not concern itself much with death. But the post-war poets have been un-usually preoccupied with death. The following lines from Eliot's "Whispers of Immortality" have been frequently quoted as offering a clue to the temper of the new poetry:

> Webster was much possessed by death
> And saw the skull beneath the skin . . .

Add to this the key in which death is dealt with in *The Waste Land*, in *The Hamlet of A. MacLeish*, and in the famous scene in Joyce's *Ulysses*. The irony on this theme quickly passes into desperation.

A different and younger school of the new poets, pri-marily concerned as we shall see with social reconstruc-tion, nevertheless in its own way evidences the same preoccupation. The following bit of light verse on the theme of death by W. H. Auden illustrates the ironical detachment of which Riding and Graves speak. The poem is entitled, "Blues (For Hedli Anderson)."

Ladies and gentlemen, sitting here,
Eating and drinking and warming a chair,
Feeling and thinking and drawing your breath,
Who's sitting next to you? It may be Death . . .

[4] *A Survey of Modernist Poetry*, pp. 224, 225. On Riding and Graves, see appendix, p. 248. Incidentally, we note how this passage belies their pretension of counting unimportant the time spirit in poetry.

Death is a G-man. You may think yourself smart,
But he'll send you to the hot-seat or plug you through the
   heart;
He may be a slow worker, but in the end
He'll get you for the crime of being born, my friend.

Death as a doctor has first-class degrees;
The world is on his panel; he charges no fees;
He listens to your chest, says—"You're breathing. That's bad.
But don't worry; we'll soon see to that, my lad."

Death as a teacher is simply grand;
The dumbest pupil can understand.
He has only one subject and that is the Tomb;
But no one ever yawns or asks to leave the room.

So whether you're standing broke in the rain,
Or playing poker or drinking champagne,
Death's looking for you, he's already on the way
So look out for him tomorrow or perhaps today.[5]

The present age thus does concern itself with death.
But Riding and Graves are right in insisting that the
treatment of this topic is not sentimental and therefore not
strictly pessimistic.[6] We have negation but not pessimism.
There is a great difference. And this applies not only to
the treatment of death in the new poetry but to the treat-

[5] *New Verse*, No. 25 (May, 1937), p. 4.

[6] Those who object that Robert Browning, for instance, among the Victorian poets dealt candidly with the subject of death may be referred to a query at this point by one of his more enthusiastic admirers of the older school, William Sharp. His attitude to death, says Sharp, "is not a novel one. The frontage is not so much that of the daring pioneer, as the sedate assurance of 'the oldest inhabitant.'" And he quotes approvingly another writer, Mortimer: "On the problem of Death, except in masquerade of robes and wings, his eupeptic temperament never allowed him to dwell. He sentimentalized where Shakespeare thought." *Life of Robert Browning* (London, 1890).

ment of life in general. Pessimism always implies evasion, irresponsibility. The view of these writers on the other hand is rather the tragic view, and the tragic view has the advantage of being clear-sighted and humble. A recent writer says apropos of T. E. Hulme, one of the influential predecessors of the present generation: "Boastfulness, sentimentalism, cynicism, and despair are equally foolish; the tragic view makes for a deep sense of personal responsibility, but never for self-pity or bravado. 'Blessed are the poor in spirit, for theirs is the kingdom of Heaven.'" He then adds, "The tragic view becomes Christian only when the redemptive and penitential motif is added, as for example in T. S. Eliot; but whatever its many guises may be, it seems to offer us the key to the most sensitive and profound art of our time."[7]

Most of the new poets escape the sentimental mode though all have not passed from cynicism and despair. Their negation frequently is that of the tragic view. From this it is not a long step to the Christian position. Is it not, however, sentimentalism in Christians that too often delays this last advance?

The essential Christian position, though it share the clairvoyant realism of the tragic view, must go beyond it. It does not pass through the labyrinth of contemporary evil to end in negation. Like the tragic view it accepts responsibility in the midst of evil, but unlike the tragic view it is aware of redemptive forces of enormous urgency present through the whole texture of existence. It counts on these on the ground of historical precedent and on the

[7] Dixon Wecter, "Hulme and the Tragic View," *The Southern Review,* Vol. V, No. 1 (Summer, 1939), pp. 151, 152.

ground of private demonstration. The disbeliever says: Very well, you have received grace and I have not! But the Christian replies: There is such a thing as "responsibility for religious belief." Those barriers that prevent the acquisition of scientific truth and aesthetic taste have their parallels in the spiritual realm. The modern mind has done much to discern the avenues to participation in art and science, and to recognize the subtlety of the personal factors involved. Why should not the capacity for religious apprehension depend upon even more drastic and rigorous self-analysis? Negation in the form of pessimism or bitterness is far from fulfilling the conditions of religious insight. Negation in the form of the tragic view is not far from the kingdom of Heaven.

When we look to the work of the writers of today and inquire as to the factors making for negation, we find for one thing the evidence of changed views of the self. The conclusions of many of the influential psychologists of our time have been widely accepted and have been decisive in the outlook of many in shaking what confidence they had in human freedom, stability and survival. The non-rational elements in personality have been more clearly recognized, and it has frequently been claimed that they have the largest role in our behavior, and this by over-riding rather than by energizing and serving the conscious self. The realities that attract many of the artists of today as the raw materials of art are not persons so much as the irrational and blind and mighty forces that appear to make a plaything of the conscious will. Artists are concerned with a dramatis personae not of persons but of sub-personal forces.

Once a year, at Darjeeling in Nepal, before the Buddhist temple, devil dances are performed. These dances by the Nepalese, wearing for the most part masks representing fiendish daemons and animals, portray the banishment of the ancient animistic powers by the incoming Buddhist missionaries. As the dance pantomime becomes more agitated one feels that the contemporary Nepalese have disappeared and that the aboriginal horde of terrors have taken their place. So the modern artist sees submerged passions as the true actors in the critical moments of our civilized life. Not the dancers themselves but the daemons are the true agents. O'Neill is concerned with disclosing in some of his plays the subhuman forces under the surface in the individual, as in *Emperor Jones* and *The Hairy Ape*.

MacLeish has a very successful example of this kind of theme in his poem, "The Tea Party."[8]

> You know, I never set with my back
> To a room, said Mrs. Markle. Fac',
> She said. I sort o' feel, she said,
> There might be somethin' there—not dead
> Spirits, she said, but somethin' alive—
> With claws.— So there they sat, the five
> Comfortable women around the kettle
> Sipping their tea while the cheerful metal
> Shone in the sun.— With claws, said she,
> And dipped her bread in her cup of tea.

[8] *Streets in the Moon*, p. 67. For another and contrariwise positive statement of this theme, the reader is referred to J. C. Powys, *A Philosophy of Solitude*, pp. 108 ff.

You feel it breathin' on your neck,
Sniff! Sniff! she said.— And Mrs. Beck
Said Don't, too loud!— And
                                    naked as apes,
Naked and hairy, primeval shapes
Circling a wood-fire, sit the five
Deep in a forest. Thin clouds drive
Dragging across the moon. An oak
Screams in the wind. The wet wood smoke
Blinds. And behind in the rustling dark
Night birds scream terror, baboons bark
And are suddenly silenced—and something creeps,
Creeps from the shadow—huddles—leaps—

La's sake, Mrs. Markle, you're spillin' your tea,
Said Miss Mapes. What on earth does the woman see!

By a somewhat different road D. H. Lawrence's intuitive
approach to persons had led him to a similar disregard for
the superficial and apparent individuality, and to an insistence on (to quote Mr. Aldous Huxley) "those mysterious forces of otherness which are scattered without, and
darkly concentrated within, the body and mind of man."
Mr. Huxley in his introduction to *The Letters of D. H.
Lawrence*, draws attention to a highly revealing letter by
Lawrence on this subject. Lawrence repudiates the treatment of the older novelists—the fitting of consistent characters into a particular moral scheme as the basis of interest in the novel, as in Turgenev, Tolstoy, Dostoevsky.
"You mustn't look in my novel for the old stable ego of the
character. There is another ego, according to whose action
the individual is unrecognizable, and passes through, as it
were, allotropic states which it needs a deeper sense than

any we've been used to exercise, to discover are states of the same single radically unchanged element. (Like as diamond and coal are the same pure single element of carbon. The ordinary novel would trace the history of the diamond—but I say, 'Diamond, what! This is carbon!' And my diamond might be coal or soot, and my theme is carbon.)"

It is well known that some of the most influential innovators of today were greatly influenced by their meeting with the new psychology, as it is loosely called, in their student days. Thus both Eliot and Conrad Aiken are said to have met with the new developments at Harvard shortly after the war, as was the case with Gertrude Stein, who made experiments of some length in automatic writing. But we have only to look at the literature. There is no question that the flood of light thrown on the springs of human action by Freud, Jung and others has greatly added to the insight especially of recent writers of fiction. It is difficult to distinguish the judicious and the excessive in these new judgments. One large field where the self is depreciated in favor of the irrational is in the use of the "stream of consciousness" method in narrative. The personal control of one's thought and life is here most often implicitly denied. As a matter of fact should we not agree that true stability of personality is rare, and that we have here one field in which the new writers are truly more realistic than the old. It may well be that especially in the conditions of life today not only poets and artists but large strata of their audience suffer from a greater degree of dissociation than in most times. Thus the observations of the psychological clinics and laboratories rightly point to the control of men by the impulses of the unconscious. This is not, however, to agree that human personality normally lacks integrity, freedom and survival.

Prof. Jung touches on these issues in his recent lectures on *Psychology and Religion.*[9] "It is, to my mind, a fatal mistake to consider the human psyche as a merely personal affair and to explain it exclusively from a personal point of view. Such a mode of explanation is only applicable to the individual in his ordinary everyday occupations and relationships. If, however, some slight trouble occurs, perhaps in the form of an unforeseen and somewhat extraordinary event, instantly instinctive forces are called up, forces which appear to be wholly unexpected, new, and even strange. They can no longer be explained by personal motives, being comparable rather to certain primitive occurrences like panics at solar eclipses and such things . . . As a matter of fact, we are always living upon a volcano and there is, as far as we know, no human means of protection against a possible outburst which will destroy everybody within its reach." Jung speaks farther on of the precariousness of consciousness in relatively primitive societies. "One of the 'perils' of the soul is, for instance, the loss of a soul." The implication is, the instability of even the civilized psyche.

Such analysis and the dissociative pressures especially of sophisticated urban life lead some of the poets to a preoccupation with the phenomena of the self and its masquerades. Here Mr. Conrad Aiken is of special interest.

[9] New Haven, 1938, pp. 16, 19.

CHAPTER VI

MR. CONRAD AIKEN AND THE SELF

This writer[1] gives evidence of a primary curiosity concerning the meaning of selfhood or identity. This topic is to him both an area of imaginative creation—the ceaseless "masquerade in differentness," the myriad evanescent postures of the dancer; it is also an urgent and desperate search for sound ground and substantial encounter in the ghostly traffic of the soul. In the poem, "Priapus," the meeting of lovers is indicated as a mockery: it is a meeting of ghosts; the self is unsubstantial and the loved one is but a reflection of the self. The figure used is that of the diver who dives to meet his own image and passes through it: a solipsistic experience. In the "Prelude for Memnon V" the theme is the "whirling You unknown," and the despair at not being able to touch the object, the *ding an sich*, or to find the right word or name or true symbol for it. Ever recurrent is the preoccupation with "individuation." Is there a balance between identity and changeableness? "Semper mutandis plus semper fidelis?" In any case,

> there is nothing
> So suits the soul as change.

Mr. Houston Peterson was so impressed with this aspect of Aiken's work that he entitled his study of it, *The Melody*

[1] On Aiken, see appendix, p. 242.

of Chaos.[2] Chapters in it are entitled, "The Vicissitudes of the Ego," and "Which is I?" We are so much impressed with the representative significance of this theme in Aiken that we shall explore a section of the *Preludes for Memnon*[3] particularly. We venture the thesis that what this poet has expressed so poignantly, though it be highly intellectual, is a main spiritual dilemma if not jeopardy of our time. It is no wonder if alongside the sense of dissociation of the self, we find lines indicative of insecurity and dismay, such as,

> For there are dark streams in this dark world, lady.
> Gulf streams and Arctic currents of the soul. (p. 6)

Mr. Aiken's work appears at a number of points to be revealing of the state of mind of the "hallucinated and depersonalized city-dweller" of today. His sensitiveness of response has enabled him to register those moods of bewilderment not to say hypnosis which the stony face of the city casts upon its multitudes. And his psychological training and curiosity together with his gifts as a poet have designated him as one to use these moods as the materials of the imagination.

There is no doubt that there is a close connection between the degree of dissociation of the modern urbanite and his despair and negation. The first effect of a lack of integration of the self is to induce a sense of unreality and remoteness in all the experiences of the world and of people. Such moods result from any form of uprootedness as we shall see in our next chapter. The consequent state

[2] New York, 1931.
[3] New York and London, 1931.

of isolation, unreality and illusion, the cult of immediate sensation seeks to beguile. For stimulants, sexual excitement and forced conviviality and hilarity, or these things reached in a merely reflected form through entertainments of screen and stage, have the virtue of giving the isolated and haunted individual a momentary if specious sense of identity and reality. There are many different levels at which modern jazz music is enjoyed, and there are those for whom it is a subtle and highly resourceful art in no way to be deprecated. But its peculiar appeal to the great numbers is its capacity through a pronounced primitivism to dissipate for a time the incubus of unrelatedness and apprehension which the modern carries around with him. These moods, then, serve to corroborate the teachings of psychology as to the instability of the self. When they are intense the subject's sense of unreality reaches the stage of hallucination or hysteria. In the midst of city throngs he knows himself rather as a phantom or a ghost, so far is he cut off from organic relation to his kind. And the sense of unreality carries with it a torturing sense of insecurity—indeed explains that special character of horror which, according to some, the world presents for the modern mind since the time of Poe and Baudelaire, the first moderns.

It becomes evident what a promising area of experience is here offered to the poet and the artist, for such victims live continually in a penumbra of phantasy and morbid sensibility, as well as changeable moods. If then we find in Aiken the juxtaposition of dissociation with negation and dismay we will not be surprised to find it elsewhere.

The anguish of *The Waste Land* is indicated by the Greek lines on the title page:

> . . . Sibyl, what is your desire? And she answered,
> My desire is to die.

But *The Waste Land* in method and in subject matter is built up upon what Mr. Tate calls the major premise of Eliot, "that the integrity of the individual consciousness has broken down." Mr. Tate points to the same malady in discussing the tragic life of Hart Crane: "Crane's biographer will have to study the early influences that confirmed him in narcissism, and thus made him typical of the rootless spiritual life of our time."

To return to Aiken's *Preludes*—we find recurrently the theme of the unconnectedness of experience. The stream of consciousness flows and one object or another colors the mind, indifferently.

> Winter for a moment takes the mind . . .
> Only for a moment; as spring too might engage it . . .
> Or summer . . . or autumn . . . (p. 3)

The present author ventures to illustrate this by lines of his own to illustrate the same theme, *here* on the moral side: the theme of the essential meaninglessness of the soul's history:

> . . . For no substantial being is ours.
> We glass the deep abysses blind,
> And there the flare of Tophet lowers
> Where late the Seven Candles shined.
> We traverse suns and moons in sleep,
> And guard no records of the deep.

Such a mood is the precise opposite of that conveyed by the aphorism of Bloy we have cited, *Souffrir passe, avoir souffert ne passe jamais.* Bloy's theme is that there is a self to profit by experience. So Nanak: "I have consulted the nine regions of the earth. Having turned my heart into a boat, I have searched in every sea. I have dwelt by rivers and streams, and bathed at the sixty-eight places o pilgrimage." But in the passage cited from Aiken the self is reduced to a passive and unaffected mirror of experience, or, more commonly, denied even that stability. This denial of the soul, the substantial and persistent self is frequently met with in contemporary literature. One theme of *The Waste Land* is that of the myriad dispersals of the self through the world. "The integrity of the individual consciousness has broken down." We may say that this doctrine of the new poets is an error but that it has this to justify itself: that the self is but unstably achieved in most men; the "will," that is, the nucleus of personality is but adumbrated. D. H. Lawrence, in one of his letters, puts the case at its worst: "It seems to me, if one is to do fiction now, one must cross the threshold of the human people . . . I realize *how* many people are just rotten at the quick." To the degree that this is the case life is experienced essentially passively, and the poet is the one who feels and expresses this clearly as here. This situation, moreover, easily leads to views of determinism and fatalism. Where the self is firmly established, when the personality is matured, the above reaction is precluded, except as an occasional exaggeration. Yet we can only speak relatively of personality as matured. Even the Christian doctrine of man characterizes him in Dante's words as

entomata in difetto,
si come verme, in cui formazion falla,[4]

imperfect larvae. But the impermanence of the self as
these poets see it is a different matter. We are reminded
of Jung's phrase quoted above concerning the primitives,
"One of 'the perils of the soul' is . . . the loss of a soul."
The Christian, however imperfect he sees the self, asserts
its value, identity and survival. For him, the self instead
of merely enduring experience passively, *reads* and im-
presses and interprets it. On the other hand, the typical
Hindu mystic is in the position of him whose "will" is but
feebly adumbrated, whose personality has not taken on
relief. His sense of the self therefore resembles that of the
poets we are considering. We see one cause for the attrac-
tion the Upanishads and other Eastern scripture exert
upon certain types of modern consciousness. The Hindu
mystic's denial of personality, his pantheism, Maya doctrine and fatalism (though these take various forms and
are not always found together) contrast with the outlook
that follows upon the Hebrew-Christian affirmation of the
individual.

We are led to examine the lines of Aiken above, "Winter for a moment takes the mind," etc., more closely because of the further relations suggested to Eastern psychology. In its context in this poem and the following ones
the passage has a very precise and very interesting sense.
Aiken is saying that the "mind" that "takes" what is given
it is not really continuing and self-identical mind. It only
becomes "mind," that is it only becomes a *self* in the

[4] "Imperfect insects, even as the grub in which full form is wanting,"
Purg. X, 128, 129.

moment of compounding with the external world, which itself is chaotic as we shall see, until caught up into the experience of, say, "winter," or "summer." The self then only comes alive in such moments. As Aiken expressly says: "And this is you!" But the successive moments in which this identification is felt are apparently disconnected and incommensurable.[5] For Aiken the self has no experience, no bloodedness, until it has read itself in "the tragic, the distorting mirror" of the non-self:

> Here is the God who seeks his mother, Chaos . . .
> > the icicle
> That woos the rose. . . (p. 5)

When Aiken says, "And this is you!" we seem to hear a deliberate echo of the "That art thou" of the Upanishads, especially as the allusion to icicle and rose reminds us of the Eastern coupling of crystal and red hibiscus. But the identifications are not the same. The pantheist of the words "that art thou" is recognizing his oneness with the world soul or universal self, and is denying as illusion any sense of selfhood into which the appearances of the empirical life lead him. But the thinker of the *Preludes knows himself* precisely in such momentary "illusions," an unstable compound,

> An emanation of emanations, fragile
> As light, or glisten, or gleam, or coruscation,
> Creature of brightness, and as brightness
> > brief. (p. 4)

[5] Here is where Wordsworth's similar conception of the creative role of the imagination with external reality differs: the imagination lives by what it sees and what it half-creates, but the continuing identity of the soul is assumed.

Thus in both philosophies the self is unreal, but in different ways. In the Upanishads the mortal self is unreal in its feeding upon time and sense experience. For Aiken's "Prelude" there is no continuing self, but only a capacity which now and then meeting with its mother, Chaos, strikes out a momentary spark of awareness. Thus Aiken, if we may imagine him speaking for himself in the *Preludes*, falls into the illusion denounced by the Sankhya school in India of confusing the practical with the metaphysical ego, even though it be only in brief moments.

A true analogy to Aiken's conception is that of the celebrated passage from the Chinese philosopher Kwang-Tze:

> Once upon a time, I, Chuang Tzu, dreamt I was a butterfly, fluttering hither and thither, to all intents and purposes a butterfly. I was conscious only of following my fancies as a butterfly, and was unconscious of my individuality as a man. Suddenly, I awaked, and there I lay, myself again. Now I do not know whether I was then a man dreaming I was a butterfly, or whether I am now a butterfly dreaming I am a man.

For Aiken likewise recognizes successive empirical identities, while cognizant of their ambiguity.

Aiken makes the precise affirmation condemned by the Sankhya school in saying:

> And you because you think of these, are both
> Frost and flower, the bright ambiguous syllable
> Of which the meaning is both no and yes. (p. 4)

Note how G. F. Moore alludes to this image in the following passage, in which he summarizes the Sankhya criticism:

The source and substance of the mystery of life, the ground of the endless succession of re-births, is that the soul confounds itself, the true self, with the empirical self thus constituted, mistakenly imagining that it is actor or sufferer in the tragedy of existence, as though a crystal on which the image of a red hibiscus flower falls should deem that it was itself red.[6]

Thus Aiken's thesis in the *Preludes*, while it resembles the view of the Taoist Kwang-Tze, differs from the characteristic position of Indian religious philosophy.

In any case, the basic point we have wished to make is the invalidation of the stable personality in these poems. From such a premise it is of interest to observe what solution the writer makes of the problem of the self, and how it compares with the certain psychologies of the East. We will have occasion to return to this theme in connection with the work of Jeffers and others.

[6] G. F. Moore, *History of Religions,* I (New York, 1922), p. 320.

CHAPTER VII

SOCIAL REALISM

The modern mind feels rightly or wrongly that it has a disabused understanding of society not possessed by former times and this too makes for negation in its view of life. In part this is due to participation in the World War and its sequel of these last twenty years. In part it is due to the sharper focus with which we now look upon the workings of our social and political institutions. Society is seen more in terms of a jungle with an external appearance of cooperation and law. No doubt thoughtful men in the nineteenth century, in the light of the Napoleonic Wars and the industrial revolution had similar reason for pessimism. But the contemporary realist feels that the demonstration is on a grander scale and that its grasp is unclouded by former idealistic or religious self-deceptions. Traditional views of human community have been immensely discounted by the Marxian analysis of its forces. And the workings of human nature appear more clearly exposed in the contemporary economic structure than heretofore.

The character of this system and its effects on culture are thus summarized by Berdyaev. "In our new period culture . . . is at the point of transforming itself into a civilization, at all points secularized, concerned with power and well-being, and dominated by a naïve realism.

Civilization is the extreme limit of the mechanization of human life and of nature. Here all that is organic dies. Mechanism, fruit of the power of human science, enslaves not only nature, but man. The latter is no longer the slave of nature; he is emancipated from its organic power, but he becomes the slave of the machine, a prisoner of the social milieu that it has created. And in civilization, the end-result of humanism, the human image begins to be effaced. Culture can no longer struggle against the growing power of civilization."[1]

The institutions of society come in for savage treatment from some of the new poets. We think of Jeffers' envenomed scorn for men in their conventional social aspects, for the law of the tribe, for codes, courts and sheriffs. "Give Your Heart to the Hawks" is the counsel given to the fratricide to commit his case to the Furies and not to the lawyers. Or we think of James Joyce's Rabelaisian, enormous satire on the church in *Ulysses*. Not only the proletarian and social revolutionary poets but others more moderate are vocal about "the deliquescence of bourgeois society,"—its coercions under the semblance of law and order, its immanent conflicts, its mediocrity of motive, lack of vitality, complacence, sordidness, obtuseness, unimaginativeness. And this carries with it a sardonic impatience with all aspects of the so-called higher life of society today, that is, its churches, its academic institutions, its art, its democracy, and its philosophy.

We are not so much concerned here with the revolutionary message of these poets as with the evidence of their disillusion and negation. What do they see of in-

[1] *Esprit et Liberté* (Paris, 1933), pp. 239, 240.

humane and debasing? How far are they right or wrong? What religious or ethical issues are involved? On the one hand the purely secular or aesthetic approach of the artists may be blind to secret and recreative processes in society upon which the religious man counts. On the other hand the poets and artists may well view the havoc of the world with a sensitiveness that has much to teach.

As regards the somberness of mind of those that have met the war conditions of our epoch at first hand, we may turn to some of the poems of W. B. Yeats, *Meditations in Time of Civil War*.[2] One poem, "The Road at My Door," tells how after conversation with Irregulars who speak lightly of civil war he turns to his chamber,

> caught
> In the cold snows of a dream.

And in the next poem, after enumerating outrages and bloodshed of the neighborhood, he broods in lines that are a sentence upon the whole world today,

> We had fed the heart on fantasies,
> The heart's grown brutal from the fare;
> More substance in our enmities
> Than in our love . . .

Paul Valéry, one of the two or three greatest poets of this century has eloquently expressed the feeling of thoughtful men with regard to the tendencies after 1918 as follows: "But it seems as if the experience (of the war) were not enough. Some place their hope in a renewal of

---

[2] *Collected Poems* (New York, 1937), pp. 231 ff. On Yeats, see appendix, p. 238.

the carnage. They find that there has not been enough distress, disillusionment, not enough disaster and weeping, not enough cripples, blind, widows and orphans. The trials of peace cause the atrocities of war to fade, despite what dread images of it are still here to appal us . . .

"What an incredible situation! Or rather what an incredible breed of men that can nurture such designs! Fully conscious, with complete lucidity, in the face of frightful memories, amid uncounted graves, those throes hardly concluded, beside laboratories where the enigmas of tuberculosis and cancer are passionately attacked— men can none the less still conceive of playing the game of death.

"Balzac, just a hundred years ago wrote, 'Without taking time to dry its feet bathed in blood up to the ankles has not Europe always recommenced war?'

"Must one not say that mankind for all its lucidity and capacity to reason clearly is incapable of sacrificing its passions and hatreds to its better knowledge, and acts like a swarm of insensate and wretched insects drawn impotently to the flame?"[3]

The Hamlet of A. MacLeish is a poem which, like *The Waste Land*, in oblique symbolism presents not one but all the maladies, not one but all the influences, that distracted and haunted the war generation in the early and middle twenties. The frightening corners of the mind, the blank silence of the stars, the lacerations and ambiguities of sex, the eerie Odysseys and Anabases of the soul, the necessity of lending ourselves to the hollow procedure of the world—all these are here, and behind much of it the

[3] *Regards sur le monde actuel* (Paris, 1931), pp. 212-214.

experience of MacLeish the ex-soldier. This feature is not explicit save in a few lines,[4] but the whole theme of the poem is the curse that lights upon us from our fathers, from the past: Hamlet coerced by his father's ghost to carry on old feuds; youth not free but the slave of an ancient ill. So we find on the title page,

No man living but has seen the King his father's ghost. None alive that have had words with it. Nevertheless the knowledge of ill is among us and the obligation to revenge, and the natural world is convicted of that enormity. . . .

A decade later the same author in his verse play for radio, *The Fall of the City* gives us the mood of a helpless society awaiting the Dictator,

Here in this city the wall of the time cracks . . .

They are milling around us like cattle that smell death . . .

They're boiling around us like mullet that smell shark . . .

At a more superficial level we may illustrate the disillusionment of today with an unquestioning patriotism by the following:

The small boy finds his jerseys small for him:
and we have outgrown our patriotic fauna
with their St. Vitus behaviour,
seeing beyond our noses
a land never to flow with milk and honey,
but winter a stonethrow (sic) off and no more roses.[5]

---

[4] Cf. also, "The Too-Late Born" in *Collected Poems*.
[5] Kenneth Allott, "Poem," in *New Verse*, No. 25 (May, 1937), p. 11.

But this generation has seen war not only on the battle-
field but also, undeclared, in the fierce acquisitiveness
and mutual preying of group on group within the community. When Dante is in Jupiter, the planet that stands
for justice, he pleads in his prayer to the chivalry of
heaven:

> Già si solea con le spade far guerra;
> ma or si fa togliendo or qui or quivi
> lo pan che il pio padre a nessun serra.[6]

This situation is apt today not only in view of blockades
and invasions where civilians, women, children suffer, but
in view of any economic policies that force other groups
or peoples into misery.

Muriel Rukeyser in her volumes of poetry, U.S.1,[7] gives
chapter and verse from a Congressional Investigation of
the "Gauley tunnel tragedy" where silicosis resulted from
the digging of the tunnel.

> Almost as soon as the work was begun in the tunnel
> men began to die among dry drills. No masks.
> Most of them were not from this valley . . .
> The ambulance was going day and night,
> White's undertaking business thriving and
> his mother's cornfield put to a new use.
> "Many of the shareholders at this meeting
> were nervous about the division of the profits . . ."

[6] Once it was the wont to make war with swords
  now it is made by withholding, now here, now there,
  the bread the tender father bars from none.
        Paradiso XVIII, 127-129, trans. *Temple Classics*.
[7] New York, 1938.

Mr. Griswold. "A corporation is a body without a soul."

Mr. Dunn. When they were caught at it they resorted to the methods employed by gun-men, ordinary machine-gun racketeers. They cowardly tried to buy out the people who had the information on them.

Mr. Marcantonio. I agree that a racket has been practised, but the most damnable racketeering that I have ever known is the paying of a fee to the very attorney who represented these victims . . .

Sixty-five pages of the volume are given to this horror and from the records, the personal testimonies, and the poetic evocation of the personal angles, we have a kind of *Case of Sergeant Grischa* in peacetime, throwing its ominous indictment from top to bottom of society. In a similar way such a play as *Tobacco Road* shows how literary materials can be used to dramatize the weak spots in the common life. Mr. Erskine Caldwell responding, in the dramatic section of the *New York Times*, to denunciation of the play by fellow Georgians, especially one of its Representatives, wrote: "I hold just as much love for the South and for my native state of Georgia as does Congressman ———. It is because I have this love that I insist upon such a story as 'Tobacco Road' as a means of exposing the shame of its civilization . . ." This motive is a persistent one in the type of poetry of which we are speaking.

Evidently the onus of the charge often falls on the powerful classes, but the deeper negation is found where all men are charged with rapacity or sordidness or vanity:

The man who'd not be seduced, not in hot youth,
By the angel of fools, million-worshipped success . . .

Has humbled himself to beg pleasure . . .
Whoever has discerned the vanity of water will desire wind.[8]

So William Blake in his Everyman, *The Gates of Paradise*, shows Youth mounting a slight ladder that pitches from the darkened earth toward the moon, and the legend is, "I want. I want."

The group of poets that has the center of interest in England today is one that is giving expression to the theme of social revolution. Their satire of contemporary life is full of wit and much of it is not more than clever lampooning. But the motives are deeply serious and now and again indignation or some other intensity raise the outcries to the level of true prophecy or lyricism. These are young men who have matured in the twenties in a Britain in jeopardy, a Britain of unemployment and wretchedness, and a Britain that they think inflexible and blind. Here is none of the profound negation and psychologizing of their predecessors. Nor is their work obscure or particularly rebellious in form. They write usually with a dry, staccato, clipped utterance which abjures "poetics" or sentimentalizing. They satirize continually the alleged complacency of the middle and upper classes. And this carries with it a protest arising out of the feeling that a great deal of traditional verse is written out of all too comfortable circumstances. There is a large amount of literature which people see with new eyes once the iron of poverty has entered into their souls. Thus, rightly or wrongly, Day Lewis satirizes the old poem of Marlowe,

> Come live with me and be my Love,
> And we will all the pleasures prove

[8] R. Jeffers, *Cawdor*, p. 16.

That hills and valleys, dale and field,
And all the craggy mountains yield.

There will we sit upon the rocks
And see the shepherds feed their flocks,
By shallow rivers, to whose falls
Melodious birds sing madrigals . . .

Mr. Lewis brings this down to date with the appropriate modifications:

Come, live with me and be my love,
And we will all the pleasures prove
Of peace and plenty, bed and board,
That chance employment may afford.

I'll handle dainties on the docks
And thou shalt read of summer frocks:
At evening by the sour canals
We'll hope to hear some madrigals.

Care on thy maiden brow shall put
A wreath of wrinkles, and thy foot
Be shod with pain: not silken dress
But toil shall tire thy loveliness.

Hunger shall make thy modest zone
And cheat fond death of all but bone—
If these delights thy mind may move,
Then live with me and be my love.

The social realism of this group leads them to feel that the present order in Britain and Europe is doomed. Whatever the good disposition of the dominant classes within a limited circle, they are paralyzed by long habits of

evasion and self-regard so as to be unable to exercise due
humaneness beyond that circle, and history prepares its
revenge. The following illustrations are from W. H.
Auden's *On This Island*:[9]

The expert designing the long-range gun
To exterminate everyone under the sun,
Would like to get out but can only mutter;—
"What can I do? It's my bread and butter." (*Poem XVIII*)

And here is the explanation of the judgment:

"Know then, cousin, the major cause of our collapse
    Was a distortion in the human plastic by luxury produced,

Never higher than in our time were the vital advantages . . .
Believed machines to be our hearts' spontaneous fruit . . .

While the disciplined love which alone could have employed
        these engines
Seemed far too difficult and dull, and when hatred promised
An immediate dividend, all of us hated . . ." (*Poem XVII*)

In the United States there is a small group of proletarian writers, in this case men who come right from the
ranks of the workers, who express the same themes, with
even more disregard for the older forms. We shall speak
of them at a later point. Much of the work of these revolutionary poets that we have mentioned is evidently a parti-
san, sometimes an hysterical, accusation against one class
or group of classes. In any case we have testimony of social
impulses and attitudes. The ethical motivation of much of
the work is unmistakable. In the proletarian work in this

[9] New York, 1937. On Auden, see appendix, p. 244.

country we find generous passion compromised by bitterness and by the sub-Christian doctrine of man common to all the collectivisms. These poets show us the masses of workers at the mercy of incalculable economic forces; steadily demoralized by the garish seductions of our materialism; and where unemployed or irregularly employed or otherwise precariously dependent, demoralized by poverty and led to grave moods of social conflict. And yet we are reminded by these poets that there are untold capacities for fraternity in the workers, a mysticism and a reservoir of greatness that the poor always have and which can be turned to implacable sacrifices against a foe or to creative collaborations.

The justice of the warnings contained in these writers may be supported by the following citation. It helps us to understand the soulless character of wide areas of our economic life today. Prof. R. M. MacIver here brings out the absence of religious values from our present order of life in contrast with primitive society.

"In primitive life the utilitarian system is utterly undetachable from the cultural life. No device, no lore, no art, is solely utilitarian . . . In this fusion, primitive society lies poles apart from our present civilization, which has carried further than any previous one the demarcation of utility from cultural significance. In the process that brought our modern civilization into being, the land, the focus of feudal values, gradually lost most of its cultural associations and has become a marketable commodity, overpowered by the impersonal category of capital. Capital itself has grown so detached from specific ends, so purely utilitarian that it embodies itself in ageless and anonymous corporations, served by transient myriads of workers bound to them by the ephemeral nexus of cash. Finance . . . has in turn detached itself from industry, thus becoming impersonal control raised to the second power. Technology . . . devises modes of relationship between man and man that stand as remote as its own instruments and engines from any other considerations than those of sheer utility. No ceremonies salute the time clock and the steam whistle, no hierophants unveil the mysteries of the counting house, no myths attend the tractor and the reaper-binder, no dragons breathe in the open-hearth furnace. For multitudes the art of living is detached from the business of living and must find what refuge it can in the now lengthened interval between today's work and tomorrow's."[10] There are gains and losses in the social evolution indicated, but the picture presents wide areas of common life today ruled by impersonal forces.

[10] *Authority and the Individual* (Harvard Tercentenary Publications); Paper, "The Historical Pattern of Social Change," pp. 143, 144.

CHAPTER VIII

A WORLD WITHOUT ROOTS

We set ourselves to grow
In the wrong earth, and soon we had no roots.
If there's no shade beneath our foliage,
There's evidence to say why.

E. A. Robinson. Amaranth.

We may approach this matter of the negation and decadence in the new poetry from another angle. Much of
this material along with corresponding elements in drama
and fiction testify to the breaking down in modern society
of what may be called the basic organic unities necessary
to men's full health and sanity and to a true culture. These
unities are (1) that which binds man to the soil, to the
life-giving breast of mother earth; (2) that which binds
men to their clan or tribe or nation—that warm and close
sense of belonging to a social group that sustains the
individual with a sense of general security; and (3) that
which binds the sexes in their normal fulfillment in the
family. These three relationships have broken down in
modern city and proletarian life to some degree. As a
result we find a demoralization that expresses itself in
modern art. Modern metropolitan men are not well, are
not fully sane. Neither is the factory worker. How can they
be? Except for the privileged few who have a background
of character and tradition that they still maintain, and

some security, their life is too abnormal and lonely and uprooted and shallow. Their satisfactions necessarily become those of sensation. They lose the sense of continuity with the past, of deep relation with their fellows. Mr. Houston Peterson has spoken of "the hallucinated and depersonalized city-dweller." And *dissociation,* as we should expect, is the hallmark of a great deal of this new poetry and modern art. Is it any wonder that the value and integrity of personality is discounted, and that emphasis is placed on the deeper impersonal forces in the psyche? Thus the poetry shows the effects of the uprooting from the land, the herding in slums, the mechanization of existence, the tortured sensibilities, the anemic spiritual life of men far from their fundamental springs.

A preliminary statement written as a basis of discussion for the Oxford Conference on Church, Community and State (1937), with special reference to "Church and Community," included the following pointed comments on the mass disintegration of today, on what it calls, "the dissolution of the spiritual bonds and accepted organizing principles which have hitherto controlled and given meaning to the common life." One cause of this "is the large-scale character of modern life. Thus, large-scale economic organization determines where and how vast masses of the population shall live. They quit the villages for the great cities and are perpetually influencing and influenced by those with whom they have no personal contact. Owing to the size and complication of modern life, the major events are the total result of myriads pursuing their own small self-centered purposes. But no one has planned them as a whole, and they come to the individual as fate.

Personal responsibility is so widely diffused that it ceases to be felt."

In accounting for the spiritual insecurity of moderns and the signs of dissociation in their art it is difficult to isolate the factor of separation from the soil. No doubt most of the anemia and negation can be directly related to the life of the city in certain of its comparatively recent aspects. It is there that we find that special combination of sophistication and uprootedness which occasion the moods typical of this work. Isolation from nature is only one of the factors here. Nevertheless we may well believe that it is an important one. However healthy many groups and strata in city life may be, and however decadent many rural groups, it still remains true that men need the rootage in the soil for full vitality.

Who can doubt that the lack of it goes far to explain such a picture as the following:

Look left: The moon shows locked sheds, wharves by water,
On your right is the Power House: its chimneys fume gently
    above us like rifles recently fired.
Look through the grating at the vast machinery: at the dy-
    namos and turbines
Grave, giving no sign of the hurricane of steam within their
    huge steel bottles,
At the Diesel engines like howdahed elephants: at the dials
    with their flickering pointers:
Power to the city: where loyalties are not those of the family.
And now, enter:
O human pity, gripped by the crying of a captured bird wincing
    at sight of surgeon's lance,
Shudder indeed: that life on its narrow littoral so lucky
Can match against eternity a time so cruel!

The street we enter with setts is paved: cracked and uneven
    as an Alpine glacier,
Garbage chucked in the gutters has collected in the hollows in
    loathsome pools,
Back to back houses on both sides stretch: a dead-straight
    line of dung-colored brick
Wretched and dirty as a run for chickens.
Full as a theatre is the foul thoroughfare: some sitting like
    sacks, some slackly standing,
Their faces grey in the glimmering gaslight; their eyeballs
    drugged like a dead rabbit's,
From a window a child is looking, by want so fretted his face
    has assumed the features of a tortoise:
A human forest: all by one infection cancelled.
Despair so far invading every tissue has destroyed in these the
    hidden seat of the desire and the intelligence.[1]

The fact is that men are children of nature. There is an
organic bond here reaching back through ages of evolution. Men dare not depart too far from their pattern of
existence in relation with mother earth established by so
many cycles. It is not just a question of overt bodily needs;
it is more subtle than that. At least childhood must not be
weaned too soon from the organic tie with nature. This
profound relation of man is the primordial medium of his
spiritual life: witness the absolutely decisive place that
nature has in the poetry, the myths and the religions of
the race. It is out of our ancient bond and kinship with the
earth that those elations and ecstasies spring that are the
commonest themes of the poet, and which are the substance of natural religion. Man deprived of this is less than
man.

[1] Chorus from *The Dog Beneath the Skin*, by W. H. Auden and C.
Isherwood (New York, 1935), pp. 47, 48.

Yet the indurated megalopolitan today is so alien to the land that Eliot writes,

> In the pleasant countryside, there it seemed
> That the country is only fit for picnics.

No wonder he asks in the same connection,

> Where is the Life we have lost in living? (*The Rock*)

It is at this point that the work of D. H. Lawrence came as a gospel to many. Both in his poetry and in his prose work, *Twilight in Italy, The Sea and Sardinia, Mornings in Mexico,* he reminds us of the rhythms of nature and of societies living in some degree according to those rhythms. He is quoted by Merrild as follows: "It is the perfect adjusting of ourselves to the elements, the perfect equipoise between them and us, which gives us a great part of our life-joy. The more machinery intervenes between us and the naked forces, the more we numb and atrophy our own senses. Every time we turn on a tap to have water, every time we turn a handle to have fire or light, we deny ourselves and annul our being. The great elements, the earth, air, fire, water, are there like some great mistresses with whom we woo and struggle, with whom we heave and wrestle. And all our appliances do but deny us these fine embraces, take the miracle of life away from us."[2] It is the sense of need for these fine embraces and this fuller life joy, moreover, which lies back of the frequent escapes of contemporary painters into tropical

[2] Knud Merrild, *A Poet and Two Painters* (London, 1938), p. 84. On D. H. Lawrence, see appendix, p. 239.

settings. But there is no need to seek out wholly exotic
lands to rediscover the deeper rhythms of the world. A
contemporary sociologist speaking of rural life states the
matter thus: "Agriculture is founded on life processes, particularly as influenced by soil and weather and the laws of
inheritance . . . As a consequence the farmer's philosophy of life is primarily organic, whereas the city man's
philosophy usually is mechanistic. The farmer lives in a
natural world, the city man in an artificial world."

Closely tied up with this factor, however, is another.
Men are uprooted today not only as regards the soil but
also as regards the community. In rural life and in primitive society the individual is one of a group and receives
thence a psychological security which is essential to his
nature. The isolation of many in modern city and proletarian existence is a commonplace. We have spoken of it
in connection with the nightmares of lonely existence in
the city utilized by Conrad Aiken in his poetry. Lawrence
cried out as we shall see in a later chapter against "the
absolute frustration" of his "primeval societal instinct"
which he felt to be far more devastating than frustration
of the sex instinct. The impersonal character of modern
life in many areas gives men no compensation for the community life of the country which they have lost. Masses
of men are transplanted from the social and religious
communities where they were integers and have become
"cowed cyphers" in the proletariat or the city, where

> . . . the active hands must freeze
> Lonely on the separate knees.[3]

[3] W. H. Auden, *On This Island*, Poem VIII.

But this leads us to a third area in which the basic organic unities of life are sundered in modern life, that of the family. The frustrations today of the normal life of the sexes, especially in the city, have much to do with the less healthy forms of contemporary art. The danger to individual and social sanity of an unsound family institution is brought out in the following passage from *Man the Unknown*, by Dr. Alexis Carrel: "But the individual who becomes only a 'unit in a school,' or a 'unit in the herd' in some great factory, city or collectivist State, is stunted in his growth. In order to reach his real strength, the individual requires the relative isolation and the attention of the restricted social group consisting of the family." But what we see in the family is "an area of private chaos," and a reviewer adds, "family life in our culture tends to be lived unobtrusively under the feet of our economic system."

One can hardly calculate the desolation wrought in the lives of sensitive and mature moderns by the frustration of the sex relationships, and we are speaking solely of the area of personal and psychological hurts. That so much potential abundance of spirit and talent is so often turned to the second-rate expressions of artistic life—wit, novelty, pedantry, exposure, self-dramatizations, masochism, hysteria—surely often has its background in ravages done to the will, to the life force itself, by traumatic experiences in the area of sex, especially by the record of sex conflict and irreparable injustices and remorses.

Such records and ravages are in the secret lives of men and women, "not to be found," as Eliot writes

in our obituaries
Or in memories draped by the beneficent spider
Or under seals broken by the lean sollicitor
In our empty rooms.[4]

Nevertheless while we live, unless exorcized, they cast their blight on the present:

Le soleil ne peut rien contre ce qui n'est plus!

Valéry

Francis Thompson carried such a shadow out of the past and his testimony of it in "Memorat Memoria" is representative:

Come you living or dead to me, out of the silt of the Past,
With the sweet of the piteous first, and the shame of the
shameful last?
Come with your dear and dreadful face through the passes of
Sleep,
The terrible mask, and the face it masked—the face you did
not keep?
You are neither two nor one—I would you were one or two,
For your awful self is embalmed in the fragrant self I knew:
And Above may ken, and Beneath may ken, what I mean by
these words of whirl,
But by my sleep that sleepeth not,—O Shadow of a Girl!—
Naught here but I and my dreams shall know the secret of this
thing:—
For ever the songs I sing are sad with the songs I never sing,
Sad are sung songs, but how more sad the songs we dare not
sing!
Ah, the ill that we do in tenderness, and the hateful horror
of love!

[4] *The Waste Land*, lines 406-409.

It has sent more souls to the unslaked Pit than it ever will
   draw above.
I damned you, girl, with my pity, who had better by far been
   thwart,
And drave you hard on the track to hell, because I was gentle
   of heart.
I shall have no comfort now in scent, no ease in dew, for this;
I shall be afraid of daffodils, and rose-buds are amiss;
You have made a thing of innocence as shameful as a sin,
I shall never feel a girl's soft arms without horror of the skin.
My child! what was it that I sowed, that I so ill should reap?
You have done this to me. And I, what I to you? It lies with
   Sleep.

Dante often characterizes the dead that he and Virgil
meet in the Inferno as merely shades, as when they tread

sopra la loro vanità, che par persona.

But Geoffrey Scott, gripped like Thompson by the living
memory of one whom he had injured, denies this, saying,
"I felt the pulses beating in your hand":

> O hate, like love, most pitiful and void,
> How long we hear
> At night some naked eddy of your strife
> Sweep cities half destroyed,
> And at the gate your fleshy shapes appear;
> How long we feel your body in the life
> Nor know what Dante knew, whose feet
> Weighed on those souls in the eternal sleet
> And on their touchless human dress,—
> And trod on husks of emptiness.[5]

[5] *Op. cit.*, pp. 10-11.

Who will venture to say how far the devastations of such private transactions go in today's world where irresponsibility inevitably accompanies our rootless existence.

The new poetry is full of either torment or the sense of ashes with regard to relationships of the sexes:

> In love not love there never are two lovers:
> There are but two together with blind eyes
> Watching within what ecstasy love suffers.[6]

In *The Waste Land* the mood of anguish and extremity of the poem is here and there intensified by evocations of the jaded lubricity or the dismal sordidness of modern love. One of the most striking passages in the poem is the allusion to the passage in Augustine's confessions where he tells of his arrival at Carthage, "where a cauldron of unholy loves sang all about mine ears":

> To Carthage then I came
>
> Burning burning burning burning
> O Lord thou pluckest me out
> O Lord thou pluckest
>
> burning.[7]

Apart from the devastations caused by sheer lawlessness and animality, there is abundant evidence of the costs of frustration in this area largely consequent upon the character of our civilization: man "burned by the ropes of his own flesh," as a result of false sex attitudes, delayed mar-

[6] A. MacLeish, *Public Speech*, "The Second Love."
[7] Lines 307-311.

riage, or the febrile overemphasis on and exasperation of sex by commercialism and amusements. More particularly such frustration is due to paralyzing inhibitions resultant from Puritan attitudes and training. The author last quoted has expressed both the oppressions and the struggle consequent on frustrations in this area in a series of "Monologues of Repression." The following section will illustrate:

I am the marble unappeased undemonstrative statue of loneliness . . . and while I inflect my head with sympathetic attention . . . feel vanity and pride in the hollow I face . . . without features, without bulk; the terrible Narcissism of emotion, that—flung out into a place where nothing reflects it—returns to itself, in self-passionate pity, and is secret.[8]

Jung in his lectures, *Psychology and Religion,* touches on a special aspect of the topic of this chapter. He says, "The educated public, the flower of our actual civilization, has lifted itself up from its roots and is about to lose its connection with the earth."[9] As the context shows he is not thinking of the uprooting as from the land or soil but more generally. Man must find a *modus vivendi* with his living body or "somatic man" which has come down with him from so long a past and which has such elements of vitality to confer. "The educated man tries to repress the inferior one in himself, without realizing that by this he forces the latter to become revolutionary." The group Jung has in mind here evidently is not to be identified with the ascetics, though it overlaps with such. The point is there are many moderns who, whether "Puritanical" or ascetic or cerebral

[8] Charlotte Wilder, *Phases of the Moon* (New York, 1936).
[9] *Psychology and Religion,* p. 95.

or sophisticate, so mismanage their relations with the body, as to be numbered among those who have broken the basic organic unities of life. Civilization today often forces such a condition on the individual.

The breakdown of the three organic unities we have named have been seen to interact. It is in the city that they combine most powerfully to affect men's experience and view of life. Sociologists have brought these facts into relation with the declining birth rate in the population centers of large parts of the western nations, and very significantly, into relation to capitalist motivations.[10] It is to be noted that by contrast with rural life, on the whole, the individual and not the family is the economic unit in the city today. Thus our social order and its ideals are powerful factors in the disintegration that is evidenced. Modern poetry frequently makes the charges against society indicated above. But more significant still, this poetry by its very character witnesses to the rootlessness and anemia of wide areas of our common life.

It is not difficult to see that there is a sharp contradiction between the type of man created by these conditions and the ideal of autonomous, responsible personality for which classical Christianity stands. This in itself offers a motive for Christian social action, and at the same time discloses the opportunity which Christianity alone has of ministering to the peculiar malady of the modern individual, that is, dissociation.

[10] See Von Ungern-Sternberg, Eugenics Research Association Monograph IV, Cold Spring Harbor, Long Island, N. Y., p. 202.

CHAPTER IX

CONTEMPORARY PERDITION

We have looked at some of the factors making for negation in the new poets. We wish now to draw the threads
together and to go deeper in understanding their temper
and that of their time. Can we put our finger on the
peculiar malady of the moderns?

A somewhat startling term has been assigned as the key-
note of the modern spirit, the term *horror* used in a somewhat technical way. It is pointed out that the origin of
modern poetry really begins with Poe and his influence on
Rimbaud and on Baudelaire. Thence the stream of influence of the symbolists comes right down to our contemporary schools.[1] Common to all has been a profound
sense of spiritual insecurity, of alienness in the world.
Groups of men have felt this in all times. But it has a particular character of strangeness and emptiness for the modern mind. The tales of Poe are only the most popular
expressions of this mood. Poe, it is said, is the first to give
full expression to the characteristic reaction to life of modern secularized man. That is, he has the agnosticism or
positive disbelief of the modern man, his divorce from
nature consequent upon the rational, critical spirit, all the
subtle maladies that follow on the broken organic unities

[1] The ablest study of this whole movement is generally recognized to
be that of Edmund Wilson in *Axel's Castle, A Study in the Imaginative
Literature of 1870-1930* (New York, 1931). See appendix, pp. 235 and
249.

described, the special preoccupation with death, and the sense of the dangerous gulfs of the soul—all of which in the deepest levels of consciousness make for the sense of estrangement or horror. This is a strong word to use, but the reaction indicated is something different from fear and well describes the lostness of man today, and is testified to by his most significant poetry and art.

It is possible to be misled here, especially if we confine our attention to fondness for the macabre or the lugubrious or the medieval. These alone are not indicative of the mood of which we are speaking, though they are present in Poe and his followers. Before Poe and contemporary with him the romantics were characterized by fondness for mournful ruins, medieval nostalgias and ghost stories, and it goes back into the end of the eighteenth century. Indeed, the preoccupation with death or the macabre is ever recurrent. But the special feeling of the modern spirit about these is something peculiarly its own.

The metaphysical poets of the seventeenth century come the nearest to this feeling and this accounts in part for the special kinship recognized in them by our group. Apart· from the appeal of their form and their intellectual quality, they have something of the same disabused, acid world view. The contemplation of the skull on the part of the medieval monk (not its pseudo-medieval sentimentalizing), the lucidity of the metaphysical poets, and the sense of the abyss in the French symbolists, all reflect the same thing in different manners. The monks of course had a different setting for their scrutiny of death, but there were the same objectivity and depth.

This main malady or sense of alienation and lostness of

contemporary man expresses itself for one thing as a vertigo or what we have called a sense of the abyss. Without even animal faith, as a consequence of his overrationalism, he peers down the precipices of the mind, and is seized with giddiness and horror, at the same time that he is drawn to the gulf and yields to the awful fascination, as Rimbaud and Crane did in different ways. We have quoted the passage from G. M. Hopkins that bears on this,

> O the mind, mind has mountains; cliffs of fall
> Frightful, sheer, no-man-fathomed . . .

Aiken warns us to fly "the terrible infinite," from which there is "no escape, Even in sleep." Eliot speaks of the fear not of death but "of what beyond death is not death." And in *Conversation at Midnight* by Miss Millay, John explains religion by saying that

> it is utter
> Terror and loneliness
> That drive a man to address the Void as "Thou."

MacLeish's volume, *Streets in the Moon,* is full, as is his *Hamlet,* of the eery consciousness of the enigma of life. In poem after poem, though often in ironical tone, the poet stands aghast at the mystery, the "Thing Behind," *Le Secret Humain.* And his task is that of Hamlet with the ghost:

> *Question it,* . . .
> *What art thou* . . .
> And no sound.

Our present theme is best expressed by the poem, "The End of the World," which incidentally shows also the tone of mock fantasy in which the modern approaches these horrors.

Quite unexpectedly as Vasserot
The armless ambidextrian was lighting
A match between his great and second toe
And Ralph the lion was engaged in biting
The neck of Madame Sossman while the drum
Pointed, and Teeny was about to cough
In waltz-time swinging Jocko by the thumb—
Quite unexpectedly the top blew off:

And there, there overhead, there, there, hung over
Those thousands of white faces, those dazed eyes,
There in the starless dusk the poise, the hover,
There with vast wings across the cancelled skies,
There in the sudden blackness the black pall
Of nothing, nothing, nothing,—nothing at all.

Jung throws light on the theme of modern man's acute sense of "the abyss." "In most people," he says, "there is a sort of primitive *deisidaimonia* (fear of the gods), concerning the possible contents of the unconscious. Beyond all natural shyness, shame and tact, there is a secret fear of the unknown 'perils of the soul' . . . But one should realize that this fear is by no means unjustifiable . . ."[2] But this condition is especially true of modern man according to the writer. It is his view that richly elaborated religious institutions, rites, creeds, disciplines, serve the purpose of fencing men away from the unpredictable and dynamic incursions of the irrational. "But one thing is cer-

[2] C. G. Jung, *Psychology and Religion*, pp. 14, 15.

tain—that modern man, Protestant or not, has lost the protection of the ecclesiastical walls carefully erected and reinforced since Roman days, and on account of that loss has approached the zone of world-destroying and world-creating fire. Life has become quickened and intensified. Our world is permeated by waves of restlessness and fear."[3]

One form in which this sense of the abyss is felt is in the frightening sense that life does not hold together, that we stand everywhere on shifting sands, that we are playthings of some blind vortex. The poem from which the following lines are taken by one of the youngest poets has been much quoted as expressing the modern's sense of relativities:

> Now all things melt and shift in the moon's light.
> The walls before you alter. The landscape
> Alters. Familiar things
> Take unfamiliar shape . . .
>
> The knowledge you had at morning by the night
> Will cope with nothing . . .
>
> It is the moment of the whirlpool, moment
> Of the abyss where all things stream.
> O you who sleep tonight within this city!
> Think now of order, for in what's to come
> You'll learn how "be" and "seem"
> May interchange along with "plan" and "chance"
> And hear above your heads destruction dance
> On the curved roof of the universe as a drum.[4]

[3] *Ibid.*, p. 59.
[4] Archibald Fleming, Sentry's Speech from "The Destroyers," *The New Republic* (July 13, 1938), p. 273.

Men today not only feel this sense of the abyss, they are drawn toward it. To use Jung's phrase, he "has approached the zone of world-destroying and world-creating fire," and though he is afraid of it, he is also allured by it: "dominated by the lust of self-demolition." The "cult of the margin," that is, the exploitation of the dangerous twilight area of the psyche, the experimenting with drugs and all manner of exceptional and abnormal experience, is one phase of this. The classic example of this is, of course, Rimbaud. "I accustomed myself to states of pure hallucination . . . I reached the point of seeing something sacred in my mental disorders."[5] Suicide is one outcome of such obsessions with the irrational. Hart Crane's suicide by leaping from a boat in the Caribbean is partly to be explained in this way. We speak in the next chapter of romantic perdition in the new poets, where it is shown how certain forms of romanticism are essentially a form of intoxication of a destructive character.

＊   ＊   ＊   ＊   ＊   ＊   ＊

An allied expression of the modern mood is found in the special preoccupation with death. As we have said the attitude here is unique. It is not sentimental; it does not partake of the Byronic. Death is no longer approached "with all the decencies" and the proper reticences. It is

[5] *Une Saison en Enfer,* "Alchimie du Verbe" (*Oeuvres,* Mercure de France.)
"Je m'habituai a l'hallucination simple . . .
Puis j'expliquai mes sophismes magiques avec l'hallucination des mots!
Je finis par trouver sacré le désordre de mon esprit. J'étais oisif, en proie à une lourde fièvre: j'enviais la félicité des bêtes—les chenilles, qui représentent l'innocence des limbes, les taupes, le sommeil de la virginité!
Mon caractère s'aigrissait. Je disais adieu au monde dans d'espèces de romances."

treated realistically. But it is also treated with imagination. It is treated with irony, but the irony is not that of a man who is in full command of himself. It shudders.

And I have seen the moment of my greatness flicker,
And I have seen the eternal Footman hold my coat, and
    snicker,
And in short, I was afraid.[6]

Riding and Graves say of this theme, "Death, a common bourgeois conviction, is the only progressive liberal subject which the modernist poet sometimes treats without prejudice. One contemporary poet actually writes of it:

This I admit, death is terrible to me,
To no man more so naturally,
And I have disenthralled my natural terror
Of every comfortable philosopher
Or tall dark doctor of Divinity.
Death stands again in his true rank and order."[7]

One must turn to the well-known choruses in Eliot's *Murder in the Cathedral* for the most impressive evocations of death and the fear of death, managed with the aid of symbolist advances in method.

❈   ❈   ❈   ❈   ❈   ❈   ❈

Accompanying these foregoing themes we find also repeatedly the theme of the sterility of existence, the drought, the parchedness of our condition. Man in alienation from the world, the organic unities broken, inevitably

    [6] T. S. Eliot, "The Love Song of J. Alfred Prufrock."
    [7] *Op. cit.*, p. 256.

finds the relish of experience gone and worse still his spirit
dying of thirst. The poets that interpret the modern mood
are therefore

voices singing out of empty cisterns and exhausted wells.[8]

The ruling feature of *The Waste Land* landscape is its
dryness and barrenness, and the thirsted salvation is suggested toward the close in the "limp leaves" that

> Waited for rain, while the black clouds
> Gathered far distant, over Himavant

until the thunder spoke over the Indian jungle.

> Here is no water but only rock
> Rock and no water and the sandy road
> The road winding above among the mountains
> Which are mountains of rock, without water . . .

and in "The Hollow Men,"

> This is the dead land
> This is cactus land
> Here the stone images
> Are raised . . .

The corresponding symbols appear in *The Hamlet of A.
MacLeish*, the desert, dry bones, the abandoned city in
the sand, the cry of jackals.

The sense of sterility leads to a paralysis of action. The
scenes in the *Hamlet* lead on to the poignant query,

> What is it that we have to do?

[8] *The Waste Land*, line 384.

And in *The Waste Land* the banal woman monologuing in desperate tedium says,

> "What shall I do now? What shall I do?
> I shall rush out as I am, and walk the street
> With my hair down, so. What shall we do tomorrow?
> What shall we ever do?"

Auden has a poem with the same refrain. A character in Evelyn Scott's symbolist novel *Escapade* characterizes herself as "a grain of sand, wind-hurled, eon after eon, across a sphinx's face."

❋   ❋   ❋   ❋   ❋   ❋   ❋

This all goes back to the unbelief of modern man, say the religious teachers. In any case the secular mind of this new age is "without priest or ephod or terephim," as Brother George Every writes,[9] citing two passages, the first from Pound's *Hugh Selwyn Mauberley*, and the following from *The Waste Land*:

> I do not find
> The Hanged Man. Fear death by water.
> I see crowds of people, walking round in a ring.

In this last quotation, spoken by the fortuneteller, Madame Sosostris as she surveys her tarot pack, we are told that Christ cannot be found, nor any redeemer, and that the multitudes wander aimlessly. We recall the words previously quoted of Mr. Allen Tate, explaining the inability of

---

[9] In *The Student World*, Geneva, Vol. XXXI, No. 2 (1938), p. 142. Brother Every is a member of the Society of the Sacred Mission and was a reviewer of poetry in T. S. Eliot's *Criterion*.

Hart Crane to create an effective myth in America: "The age is scientific and pseudo-scientific, and our philosophy is John Dewey's instrumentalism. And it is possibly this circumstance that has driven the religious attitude into a corner where it lacks the right instrument for its defense and growth, and where it is in a vast muddle about just what these instruments are." In view of these dilemmas of faith and the havoc of today's life, many men today will agree with the following:

if there is Goodness, it should speak now . . . with or without power. I do not believe in God, until that God . . . with full complete expression of more than the straining and disappointed expectation of a benevolent hope, manifests himself.[10]

Whatever the relation of disbelief to the modern sense of estrangement and the consequent barrenness of life, a more fundamental explanation can be found. This explanation may be formulated in either of two terms. The term proposed by Berdyaev and applied by him to post-war art and poetry is "the loss of the human image" or "identity." The alternative term we would propose is that of dissociation. In either case it is held that modern man is in a condition of alienation from his veritable self, and that from this condition arise the maladies we have evidenced. Tate says of Rimbaud and Crane: "Rimbaud achieved 'disorder' out of implicit order, after a deliberate cultivation of 'derangement,' but in our time the disintegration of our intellectual systems is accomplished. With Crane the disorder is original and fundamental. That is the special qual-

[10] Charlotte Wilder, *Phases of the Moon*, p. 42.

ity of his mind that belongs peculiarly to our own time."[11] And further, "Eliot's 'pessimism' grows out of an awareness of *the decay of the individual consciousness* and its fixed relations to the world . . ."[12]

Berdyaev states this dissolution or derangement of the individual consciousness in his framework of the havoc wrought by humanism since the Renaissance. The argument will be found in his book, *The End of Our Time*. The Middle Ages represented an infinitely rich affiliation of antiquity with Christianity, and man's supreme creative hour was in the first or Christian renaissance of the thirteenth century. The contribution of antiquity was the definition of the image or identity of man, and that of Christianity was one of asceticism and energy. Thanks to the ascetic discipline of the Middle Ages man had an immense resource of creative power which has only now exhausted itself. The Renaissance signified the beginning of an experiment in humanism—"the great Christian heresy"—whose bankruptcy is only now fully evident. The humanistic experiment led via the Reformation, the eighteenth-century glorification of Reason, the French Revolution, modern science, individualism and *laissez faire* to its present bankruptcy—a demonstration that "man cannot remain man without God." The present moment is one of general disintegration. This means an age of relative barbarism pointing to the end of pure science and technology and positivism, but offering men the opportunity of a new depth of experience. The evidence for the present cultural chaos is to be seen in modern art and especially in futur-

[11] "Hart Crane," in *Reactionary Essays,* p. 26.
[12] *Ibid.,* p. 31. Our italics.

ism, with its mutilation of the human form and its subordination of the mutilated human form to chaotic elements drawn from sense experience.

What is particularly to the point here is that Berdyaev illustrates his theme from painting and poetry of today. He is proving his point that we have lost the great contribution of antiquity, that is, the human image or identity. The great achievements of Greece, the human body and the human reason are renounced by futurism. It seeks its form "neither from nature or man, but from the machine . . . The image of man, his soul and body, are lost in such art; they are broken into pieces by torrents of subpersonal forces, and nothing remains of them but fragments. The cubism of a great painter like Picasso had already dismembered the body of man and confounded his identity for art. Futurist painting . . . pushes still farther the dissociation of the human consciousness. The sharp boundaries of all natural forms are violated. One thing is merged in another and man in inanimate objects; advertisements, splinters of glass and leather soles appear with any given natural form and destroy it . . ."[13]

"The fragmentation and destruction of the divine image in man can be observed in the poetry of André Biely, one of the most remarkable artists of our time. André Biely is related to futurism, but he goes well beyond futurism. His art does violence to all natural boundaries, all static forms of creation; man and the cosmos are dissolved in savage gestures. The image and identity of man could never be found in such art. His image can no longer be distinguished from a lamp-shade, the boulevards of a city; it crumbles in

[13] Translated from *Un Nouveau Moyen Age* (Paris, 1930), pp. 52, 53.

a cosmic infinite."[14] Those familiar with recent art and literature will understand what Berdyaev refers to: the heterogeneous assortment of objects on a canvas, including perhaps a human forearm or other feature along with inanimate objects. Surrealism gives it to us with its doctrine of "pure psychic automatisms." In literature we find it in the stream of consciousness school in its extremes. Berdyaev would seem well advised in connecting such anti-personal trends in art and literature with a disintegrated culture. Winters says of James Joyce that he "endeavors to express disintegration by breaking down his form, by experiencing disintegration before our very eyes . . ." Most often this process is unconscious rather than deliberate but the result is the same.

There will be those who find Berdyaev's terms uncongenial. A Protestant will object to the inclusion of the Reformation in the series of phases that led to modern secular individualism, even though writers like Dawson and Maritain agree with Berdyaev. The Reformation did, indeed, further the dissolution of the bonds of one kind of society, and nominally Protestant forces have contributed to the irresponsibility of modern society. But the Reformation was essentially a community-building impulse as was the primitive Christianity it renewed. This was evident especially in the Calvinist wing of Protestantism. Luther and Calvin laid the stress on responsible as well as on autonomous personality. Re-emphasis on this and on the ecumenical consciousness is the order of the day in extra-Catholic Christendom. With this comment we may accept the thesis of Berdyaev.

[14] *Ibid.*, pp. 54, 55.

A less dogmatic explanation of the modern sense of alienation is in terms of dissociation. The modern urbanite is a dissociated person, and the hallmark of modernist literature is dissociation. We have reached this conclusion already by a number of paths, and we have noted the particular challenge that it presents for those forms of Christianity which conceive of man in fully personal terms.

In whatever terms we view the lostness of men today, we have evidence enough of the torments consequent upon it. This is not new. Emerson, studying the faces of the hurried anonymous throngs on Boston Common, saw them as "doomed men going to judgment." Eliot looks on the crowd that flows over London Bridge, and Dante's lines expressing consternation and compassion at the sights in the *Inferno* come to his mind,

I had not thought death had undone so many.

But modern perdition has its own particularities and its own outcries.

PART THREE. ALTERNATIVE FAITHS

I have consulted the nine regions of the earth. Having turned my heart into a boat, I have searched in every sea. I have dwelt by rivers and streams, and bathed at the sixty-eight places of pilgrimage. *Nanak.*

They . . . became vain in their imaginations, and their discernment in so far as it abandoned rationality became obscured. All the time insisting that they held the truth, they nevertheless fell into unreality, and ended by substituting for the glory of the incorruptible God the symbols of corruptible man, and even of birds and four-footed beasts and reptiles. *The Epistle to the Romans, 1:21-23, paraphrase.*

CHAPTER X

THE CULT OF THE IRRATIONAL

We have seen what negations are characteristic of the recent poetry, representing as it does a secularized and uprooted culture. It is of particular interest to inquire what affirmations this poetry makes, despite its experience of the world. As we have found in it a clue to the disbelief and despairs of its generation, it may serve as an index of what solutions are groped for today by the masses, solutions alternative to the orthodoxies rejected. Men do not continue in negation but turn to some construction of values open to them. If the values of the Hebrew-Christian tradition are closed as closed they are for long to wide strata of men today, they will necessarily look elsewhere for their world view and their cult and commerce with the ground of life. Such options in the field of speculation and religion are curiously limited and we find men in all ages of the world turning to some ancient altar.

Fortunate, indeed, if they do not turn to the dark gods of destruction. Yet this is an ever-recurrent danger. Brother George Every, speaking of the search for a modern paganism in the work of D. H. Lawrence and the *early* Yeats says: "Both hoped for a *débâcle* to destroy science and the machine, that their white minds might be delivered from the obsession of a rational and ordered world conceived by Plato and hardened by Christendom, and might follow

113

their dark hearts in an ecstasy of worship of the dark gods, the pagan powers that must return.

"In 1913 this was a romantic and decadent cult . . . But in the 1930's a great European nation has set itself to do what Lawrence conceived in 1922 and 1927 that Australia or Mexico might do. It has dismissed scientific education, philosophy, the intellectuals, and the Roman Catholic and Protestant Churches, to return to a pre-Christian cult. All those interested in the universal aspects of the German Faith Movement ought to read *Kangaroo* and *The Plumed Serpent* . . ."[1]

Fortunately the pagan religious solutions offered today include less alarming ones. The position of Yeats himself in his latest work we shall refer to later. Nevertheless, the great majority of these solutions today, whether debased irrationalisms or the nobler forms of pantheism, are non-Christian. It reflects the fact that the energies of men which so long have continued in uneasy partnership with Christianity and Judaism have today broken loose and assumed a specifically non-Christian if not anti-Christian and anti-Jewish form. It is too much to say that the church is going into the catacombs again throughout the West, but what has happened to the synagogue and the church in Germany and Russia is symptomatic of the age. It is to be noted that the forces opposing the Christian order today derive much of their strength from what elements of Christianity they have taken up. But this very debt helps to account for the animosity and blasphemy manifested for the Cross of the Christian, as well as for the Law of the

[1] "Life, Life, Eternal Life," in *The Student World*, Geneva, Vol. XXXI, No. 2 (Second Quarter, 1938), p. 139.

Jew. Nils Ehrenström has used the strange phrase, "a post-Christian society" to describe the one we live in. "The common life of mankind is increasingly being built upon a post-Christian basis; it is leaving Christianity behind it."

We need not be surprised to find that poets who abjure the religious faith of their people give evidence of some variant affirmation. We have learned that there is hardly such a thing as an atheist, as we are learning today that there is no such thing as a nation that rejects religion. The word secularism is a misnomer. The human spirit evolves religion as inevitably as the body breathes, and if one form is denied it is under the impulse of another. A rationalistic world view can only be temporary.

A notable address of Dr. Adolf Kellar at the Oxford Conference on Church, Community and State in 1937, dealt in part with the emergence of new religions in the contemporary world. He had in mind not only new religions of nationalism or communism, in Germany, Italy, and Russia, but a larger fact. The human soul, humanity itself, is as fertile and fecund in the production of religions as the tropical zone in the production of vegetation. They swarm and propagate at all times, but especially under abnormal conditions, and when the restraints of some older religious control are weakened. When the house is swept and garnished, seven other spirits worse than the departing one enter and the last state is worse than the first. And the enthusiasms, the fumes, the vapors, that possess men's minds, that alienate a whole people, or that delude the intellectual and the poet, rise from deep in the earth and deep in the race—the spirits of soil and nature, tribe and blood: what Goethe shows Faust descending through, deeper and deeper, the Mother Spirits of the Earth. Thence come all pantheisms and nature worship, all cults of the Land and the Kindred, Shinto or Aryan, and what private intoxications delude shaman or *illuminé*. Such cults and prophecies differ from corresponding features, also founded on ultra-rational impulses, in what we call high religion. In the latter the "better part" in man is the medium of the voices. The numinous speaks to him, indeed, through earth and blood, but not from mother earth alone and not from the bonds of kindred alone. The earliest Hebrew steps in high religion carried with them the stoning of the necromancer and geomancer, wizard and false prophet. And though they carried the bond of the peculiar people on into their purer faith—it was increasingly disciplined by universal claims.

When we turn to modernist poetry and try to identify and classify the various elements that may be called religion or religious philosophy we find ourselves in difficulty. Poets are not prose writers, least of all theologians. Yet even when they repudiate any personal confession in their work, it usually makes itself felt. Some are bold to be the teachers and seers and legislators of their generation. We have noted that MacLeish, in protesting against the specialized or "pure" conception of poetry and against the predictions by Edmund Wilson and others of its early demise, insists on its role as savior of the people. Where "the church cannot," poetry can persuade men of the newness and values of the future and elicit from them that "act of the spirit which is difficult." Here we have a modern poet that does not lag far behind the bards of the past in exalting his vocation. Indeed, he refers to Aristotle for his authority who said: "history draws things which have happened, but poetry things which may possibly happen." We are not far from Æ who says: "all true poetry was written on the Mount of Transfiguration, and there is revelation in it and the mingling of heaven and earth."[2] But few of our poets today would be so explicit about their role. And few, MacLeish included, are specific about their world view.

For the reasons we have indicated above and in the chapters on the factors making for negation today, we may not expect a positive theism among the affirmations we find. What affirmations are attained will come, moreover, out of the general movement of irrationalism, which is so characteristic of today. In philosophy, vitalism and pragmatism; in theology, Kierkegaard and Barth; in art, surrealism; in psychology, the incursions of the unconscious —in all, the reason is decried and men look for reality in other ways. Myths, symbols, mandalas, dreams are the best conveyers of meaning. The dynamic but dangerous and undiscriminated powers of the unconscious become the clues to reality. There is little objectivity, and even if nature be taken as object—or, as with Hart Crane, a period of history—it becomes but a mirror of romantic subjectivism, and still the voices come not from nature or history but from the unconscious, not from the outer order but from the disorder within. As Berdyaev says, the image and identity of man is lost and therewith the clear forms and identities of all things. The gods are now not only seen as relative, the plastic and intellectual creatures of different ages of man, but man now makes gods directly of

[2] Cited in Figgis, Æ (George Russell), (New York, 1916), p. 38.

the *subrational* forces of his being. But this means that man puts himself in the place of God. Jung thus concludes his discussion of the religious symbolism of the dreams of our contemporaries, "A modern mandala[3] is an involuntary confession of a peculiar mental condition. There is no deity in the mandala, and there is also no submission or reconciliation to a deity. The place of the deity seems to be taken by the wholeness of man."[4] For the secular man of today the available alternatives to theistic religion lie in the direction of irrationalism, finding their objects in the powers of the unconscious. Undoubted experiences of salvation are so attained. Modern men are convinced that they are able so to come to terms with, be adequate to, the claims made upon them by life.

It should be made clear that there are among the writers of our group some who must be set apart from the attitude we are here describing. Not only have some become Christian converts, but there are others who with all their exposure to the age have been able to maintain a humanist or rational faith. We think of the unyielding stoic integrity of E. A. Robinson. We devote a section farther on to the position of Yeats. The poets of the social revolutionary group we must dissociate throughout from the wrestlings with primitivism we are here concerned with. All of these represent points of view of masses of inarticulate men of today, but the cult of the irrational is perhaps the most significant as a cultural symptom.

To understand the more violent forms of recent art, not to say conduct and morals as well, one must realize some-

---

[3] A mandala is a religious symbol or instrument of ritual. Its character is indicative of the contents of the subconscious.

[4] *Op. cit.*, pp. 99, cf. p. 106.

thing of the revulsion increasingly felt by many minds against traditional tastes and standards. A cultural and moral atmosphere that to many of us, indeed, has seemed to have a sufficient share of oxygen has meant suffocation to them. They have found the stream of life in our age, in its traditional forms, meager, thin—a famishing fare. This applies to many areas of American cultural life, religious, educational, as well as aesthetic. Rightly or wrongly, new generations, testing what they find by what they have in their hearts, revolt. Their reaction is so convulsive and violent that it drives them to extreme expressions. There are times when such seemingly unpardonable new ventures in the arts can be justified. A French critic commenting on the Surrealist Exposition at Paris during the season of 1937-1938 praises by contrast the earlier phases of the post-war revolt in painting. "It is well known what the Dada movement represented then, that movement out of which surrealism was born: a living revolt against everything, a gesture . . . the need of crying out something, anything at all, so as not to stifle in an atrocious atmosphere. This gesture and this cry called us back brutally to essential reflexes and elementary feelings."

But the course followed by the Dada movement shows the dangers of even a pardonable plunge into the irrational. "For these artists hostile to all 'reality' and all external aids nevertheless had to find their food somewhere, and it is in the immense domain of the subconscious that they found it, in the most violent and immediate manifestations of man: the dream and the sexual instinct. And all that these 'monsters' of art have of arbitrary, cruel, paradoxical, troubled, defiant, disproportioned, even of comic, in a word of undeniable possibilities of poetic and plastic invention—enfranchised and intoxicated—was exploited with all the more eagerness that no properly human control could limit it. One could say much about this choice of a spiritual material which gives man the illusion of a transcendence and a liberation, a form of pride that looks to the self for all and to the external world for nothing . . ."[5]

This passage concludes with a very penetrating statement of the unhappy outcomes of much modern art. But note that the original impulse came from an understandable revolt against what the author characterizes as "a truly terrible banality, full of menace."[6]

It would seem that there is a basic misunderstanding in the minds of many modern poets as to the sources of art and poetry. The influence of Rimbaud and the French symbolists has led men to cultivate states of feeling or excitement somewhat artificially and in detachment from their fellows in the ivory tower. This subjectivity necessarily exploits the subconscious, the great but ambiguous

[5] Jean Bazaine, "Exposition surréaliste," in Esprit, Revue internationale, 6e année, 66 (1er Mars 1938), pp. 950, 951.

[6] Miss Harriet Monroe reviewed the first exhibition of cubist and post-impressionist paintings in Chicago in part as follows: "American art, under conservative management, is getting too pallid, moveless, photographic. Better the wildest extravagances of the cubists than the lifeless works of certain artists who ridicule them. Better the most remote and mysterious symbolism than a camera-like fidelity to appearances. We are in an anaemic condition which requires strong medicine, and it will do us good to take it without kicks and wry faces . . . Revolt is rarely sweetly reasonable; it goes usually to extremes, even absurdities. But when revolutionary feeling pervades a whole society or its expression in the arts, when the world seems moved by strange motives, and disturbing ideals, then the wise statesman, the true philosopher, is in no haste to condemn his age. On the contrary, he watches in all humility the most extreme manifestations of the new spirit, eager to discover the deeper meaning in them." A Poet's Life, New York, 1938, p. 215.

reservoir of emotion and imagination, and to exploit it in the wrong way. It is rightly insisted that thence too comes all great and constructive art. We must therefore distinguish between the right and the wrong use of the dynamic powers of the soul. The wrong use is found wherever the poet exploits his subjectivity in willful detachment from reality; where he lacks in humility, and to use Tate's words, "attempts to impose his will upon experience and to possess the world." Such a procedure while it may reach a great intensity of experience, divorces the poet from reality and furthers a personal dissociation because of its disregard for all but the abnormal functions of the self.

The final distinction lies here: beauty is to be loved, not used. Communion with the life of the world is to be sought, but not exploited by however subtle or spiritual a form of aggrandizement. Ecstasy, and that last stage of the mystic ladder, union, are worthy of all men to be desired, but they should not be confused with drunkenness. "Be not drunken with wine, wherein is excess, but be ye filled with the Spirit," has its application here. It is true that we exalt the Christian mystics who experience unutterable things:

Trasumanar significar per verba non si poria. Paradiso, I, 70, 71[7]

But mysticism worthy the name is given its whole direction and character and quality by the rationale of ideas and sentiments from which it springs. There is here something different from the Panic orgies of the glades, the Druid stupefactions of the rocky places, or the mysteries of the

---

[7] "The experience of passing beyond the limits of humanity may not be told in words."

chthonic deities of the underworld, all of which cults are still pursued.

A Note on Hart Crane
As Discussed by Yvor Winters and Allen Tate

Hart Crane was born near Cleveland, Ohio, in July, 1899 of New England stock. He was brought up in that city where his father was a confectioner, and attended the public schools through the third year of high school. Beyond that he was self-educated. He found his way to a reading of a good deal of literature, but his knowledge was very fragmentary. He became aware of the French symbolists and he pressed through that open door into the discovery of his own manner. His more important work began in the early twenties. He thought of himself as one providing "an answer to the cultural pessimism of the school of Eliot."[8] Crane's first book, *White Buildings* (1926) is made up in the main of short poems, some of them of the most amazing power, but rather the power of an obsessive dream than of waking reality. Examples may be seen in Rodman's *A New Anthology of Modern Poetry*, but the *Collected Poems* (New York, 1933) should be secured. His ambitious work, *The Bridge*, in which he takes the Brooklyn Bridge as a symbol and undertakes to write an American epic, was published in 1930. Crane died by suicide in 1932, leaping from a boat in the Caribbean.

His work is of special interest to those attentive to the directions that the religious spirit takes outside the usual

---

[8] For these facts see Tate, "Hart Crane," in *Reactionary Essays*, pp. 26-42. See also Philip Horton, *Hart Crane, The Life of an American Poet* (New York, 1937). Winters' discussion will be found in *Primitivism and Decadence*, pp. 27-33.

forms, but he is probably the most difficult of all the poets considered in this study. An example of his fascination and his difficulty is the following from that section of *The Bridge* entitled "The Dance." This section like many others draws on the figures and early phases of American history. In this case we have to do with an Indian dance. It celebrates the ultimate glory of the American spirit. For it accompanies the burning at the stake and the consequent apotheosis of a chieftain who symbolizes the land. The stanzas describe his change.

> O, like the lizard in the furious noon,
> That drops his legs and colors in the sun,
> —And laughs, pure serpent, Time itself, and moon
> Of his own fate, I saw thy change begun!
>
> And saw thee dive to kiss that destiny
> Like one white meteor, sacrosanct and blent
> At last with all that's consummate and free
> There where the first and last gods keep thy tent.

Crane was in the truest sense a romantic, but a romantic of the twentieth century. He sought his passion in his own interior life and in rebellion against rules and conventions like other romantics, but as one who belonged to the demoralized spiritual world of our time. The object on which he fixed his ardor was an undefined dream of the American future, one that fed itself partly on the technological achievement of the present, witness the central place that the Brooklyn Bridge has in its conception. His feeling for America was the more truly romantic in that his knowledge of the land and its history was so limited. Crane was a mystic and in some sense a pantheist. He was religious in his approach to his art. He conceives of his greatest poem as an attempt to give America a religious epic. All his work betrays a search after the absolute, and as Tate has pointed out, it was his inability to accept accommodation in face of reality that drove him back on sheer subjectivism and finally suicide. Crane gave himself to the cult of the irrational and it is this that occasions the present note.

This poet is the outstanding example of the influence of the French neo-symbolist poets in this country. He illustrates the two characteristics of that school: as regards style, the break with the metrical rules of classicism and with the definiteness of the image; and, far more important, as regards the whole approach to poetry, the reverence for the arbitrary deliverances of the poet's inspiration, apart from conscious or rational control. Crane's poems often have a hypnotic power about them which marks them out as among the most extraordinary performances with language to be found in American poetry. One may call it genius or one may say that he had a wholly exceptional mediumistic power to set on paper the contents of the subconscious carrying with them still a kind of inhuman quality.

Comment on Crane by Yvor Winters and Allen Tate illuminates the theme of the foregoing chapter. We will begin with a quotation from the former. Winters is here discussing the English poet T. Sturge Moore and is led to speak of the particular temptation of poets like Crane as "that spiritual pride which would overreach natural limits . . . the effort to violate human relationships by imposing one's identity on others." Winters continues, "The theme, however, is not limited to the ethical sphere in Mr. Moore, but has its religious counterpart, in a mysticism related to that of poets so diverse as Hart Crane and Robinson Jeffers, which leads to the attempt to violate our relationship with God, or with whatever myth we put in his place, even with Nothingness, and which leads concurrently to the minimizing of moral distinctions, that is, of the careful perception of strictly human experience. Mr. Moore differs from the romantic mystics in defining this temptation without succumbing . . ."[9] Thus where Moore in his poem "To Silence" can address the mystical experience,

> Yet I, who for all wisdom pine,
> Seek thee but as a bather swims
> To refresh and not dissolve his limbs,

there are others who would irremediably dissolve their limbs. This motive is fixed on as the significant feature of romanticism, as its characteristic moral defect, by Tate in the following way. Speaking of Crane he says, "From then on, instead of the effort to define himself in the midst of almost overwhelming complications—a situation that might have produced a tragic poet—he falls back upon the intensity of consciousness, rather than clarity, for his center of vision. And that is romanticism . . . Crane could only assert a quality of will against the world, and at each successive failure of the will he turned upon himself. In the failure of understanding—and understanding for Dante, was a way of love—the romantic modern poet of the age of science attempts to impose his will upon experience and to possess the world. . . . A poetry of the will is a poetry

[9] *Primitivism and Decadence*, p. 85.

of sensation, for the poet surrenders to his sensations of the object in his effort to identify himself with it, and to own it."[10]

These two quotations probe very deeply into the error of many modern artists. Note how closely they agree. In both cases the danger is a moral one, that of spiritual self-aggrandizement, the desire in the one case "to impose one's identity on others," and in the other "to impose one's will upon experience and to possess the world." This procedure is abetted in those of a mystical disposition by the secularism of today. Apart from the Roman Church contemporary religion does not present an order of faith of sufficient massiveness and authority to persuade to self-surrender. Each man must seek his own divinity in his own bosom but without the clarification and renewal that the Protestant Christian has at this point as well as the Catholic. But the divinities that the modern finds in this way are those of the irrational, prodigal of power but also of destruction.

What we are saying applies to all romantic poetry in so far as it is reckless of ultimate controls. Poets like Crane and D. H. Lawrence are romantic poets in this aspect in that it is a poetry of sensation rather than of objectivity. The consequences of such uncritical forms of passion are evident. Tate can say of Crane: "At one moment Crane faces his predicament of blindness to any rational order of value, and knows he is damned"; and Winters: "It may seem a hard thing to say of that troubled and magnificent spirit, Hart Crane, that we shall remember him chiefly for his having shown us a new mode of damnation . . ."

[10] *Reactionary Essays*, pp. 39, 40.

There are many types of romanticism—and we are speaking now rather of its spiritual attitudes than its artistic aspects. But in so far as it signifies a willful self-blinding in sensation, an immersion in mysticism or emotion that abandons the critical faculties and refuses respect for the object, in so far it is destructive.

> Lo, with a little rod
> I did but touch the honey of romance—
> And must I lose a soul's inheritance? (Oscar Wilde)

Even such a noble form as that of Wordsworth knows its penalties—the anti-climax after romantic intoxication:

> I thought of Chatterton, the marvellous boy,
> The sleepless soul that perished in its pride;
> Of him who walked in glory and in joy
> Following his plough, along the mountain-side:
> By our own spirits are we deified:
> We poets in our youth begin in gladness,
> But thereof comes in the end despondency and madness.

This is not merely the natural nostalgia for the greater vividness of youth's sensibility. It is the nemesis of idolatry. In the cases of such *poètes maudits* as Rimbaud, who deliberately cultivated the marginal life of the soul, we see the perilous experiment carried out to its limits. Rimbaud, significantly enough, sought later to return to Christianity, but its existing forms failed to offer him the aid he needed. They were too much impregnated with the toxic atmosphere of Europe that he had long been trying to escape. A truly great poet of this type, Baudelaire, was able finally to recover himself in terms of the Catholic tradition.

There are comparatively mild forms of such indulgence that do not destroy their mystics.

What distinguishes the unhealthy from the healthy mystic or pantheist is for one thing the element of courage. A Crane, as Tate shows, cannot face his predicament and "tries to rest secure upon the intensity of sensation." But this leads to despair. For another thing it is the element of reverence. The greedy romantic wishes not only to enjoy but "to impose his will upon experience and to possess the world." He wants to *use* it, and often to use it at its most sacred. The result in poetry is really a form of black magic. The true mystic while he craves for communion and furthers it nevertheless reverences its object.

Tate includes Shelley with romantics like Rimbaud and Hart Crane whose personal willfulness is frustrated by facts they refuse to admit, and who then are defeated as men and as poets. But surely Shelley is misjudged. This is evidenced by the misinterpretation of the "Ode to the West Wind."[11] "His will being frustrated by inhospitable Truth, Shelley is broken; falls into disillusionment; and asks the west wind to take him away and make him its lyre." One can only view it this way if he disbelieves in the realities to which Shelley appeals. Since when has disaster become synonymous with being broken? It is Shelley himself who teaches that hope creates from its own wreck the thing it contemplates. Shelley is not "broken," as the hope voiced in the conclusion of the poem testifies. He does not fall into disillusionment in the sense that Tate implies; but into grief. His offering of himself to the west wind is an almost exultant affirmation. The poem is written in the

[11] *Reactionary Essays*, pp. 96, 97.

first person, but it is the first person of prophecy, not that of egotism. To use Mr. Yvor Winters' terminology he wins a "moral" victory over his experience, both for life and for the discourse of the poet.

Thus while Shelley's work has an element of subjective distortion of experience, it is related to reality in a way that the work of Rimbaud and Crane is not. Nor is this judgment based merely upon a preference for the kind of philosophy that Shelley held. It is warranted, as in the case of all positive mystical and religious literature from Plato to Bridges, by the pragmatic test, in the lives of the poets under view, both in their individual mastery of the raw materials of their personal lives and in their social attitudes; all reflected in their artistic creation. Shelley's work is more implicitly mastered and coherent. If Shelley's faith was a deluded escape ending in quicksands we would have other evidence of it than *Prometheus Unbound.* A romantic who gives himself more completely to subjectivity like Crane may none the less produce a work close to genius but it will bear the marks as *The Bridge* does, of escapism that is escapism indeed: what D. H. Lawrence himself spoke of as "the awful katabolism in the abyss"; and as that falling *out* of the hands of the living God which is a more fearful thing than falling *into* those hands.

In denouncing traditionalist and idealistic poets we must then make a careful distinction. "Escapism" in them is to be diagnosed where they are found to be exploiting their subjectivity in willful detachment from reality. But this is not to be confused with a valid celebration of the experiences of the inner life. Such idealist poetry is founded on commerce with the real world of the spirit teachably explored. Mr. Tate aids us here by his distinction between poetry of the "will" and poetry of the imagination. The former seeks sensation and gratification willfully, at the expense of reality; it would "use" the mysterious and dynamic forces of the soul and not reverence them. This is the danger of much romantic poetry.

CHAPTER XI

THE NEW PANTHEISM

The loose term pantheism is the most available for characterizing as a whole the religious philosophy that comes to expression in the irrationalist group we are concerned with: D. H. Lawrence, Hart Crane, Robinson Jeffers. Pantheism is ever the great alternative to theism. But the pantheism we meet here is not by any means the idealistic type we associate with Wordsworth or Spinoza or Æ or Tagore. The view of nature that Wordsworth held is excluded for these present-day poets, as is that of Shelley or Emerson. Nature personified, or the Oversoul, or the One that remains while the many change and pass—all these are too much idealized or humanized or rationalized. The romantic pantheists read themselves into the All too easily; that is, they assign personality, spirit to it as in Æ's well-known poem, "Oversoul," whose text is cited from the Gita,

I am Beauty itself among beautiful things.

An excellent example of this kind of pantheism is afforded by a poem of James Stephens. Note that the beautiful, the sympathetic, the humanized aspects of nature are those attended to.

The Voice of God[1]

I bent again unto the ground,
And I heard the quiet sound
Which the grasses make when they
Come up laughing from the clay.

"We are the voice of God," they said:
Thereupon I bent my head
Down again that I might see
If they truly spoke to me.

But around me everywhere
Grass and tree and mountain were
Thundering in mighty glee,
"We are the voice of Deity."

And I leapt from where I lay,
I danced upon the laughing clay,
And, to the rock that sang beside,
"We are the voice of God," I cried.

The attitude of the irrationalist poets toward nature must be called, by contrast with these, a new pantheism. It is a bald naturism or elementalism which refuses ordinarily to personify, which chooses as its favorite symbols those aspects of nature that are alien to man and wild, if not cruel, and that in general dehumanizes its quest to the point of nihilism. It is true that some of these poets have brooded on the great source of most nature worship, the Upanishads, just as have men like Emerson and Æ and Whitman. But the Upanishads are protean in their teaching, and what Æ finds there to suit him is different from what Robinson Jeffers finds.

[1] James Stephens, *Songs from the Clay* (London, 1915), p. 46.

In the older scriptures of India as a whole one can distinguish two important strains among others: (1) the effort to experience a sense of oneness and identity with living nature or the Absolute pushed to an ecstatic monism, whether theistic or not; (2) a reaction against the life of the reason and a total negation of all human experience. The first of these emphases is the most characteristic. In its various forms it attracted Schopenhauer and Emerson and Shelley and Æ. One could find endless illustrations:

> There is one being only who exists,
> Who like the air supports all vital action.
> He moves yet moves not: He is far, yet near.
> He is within this universe, and yet
> Outside the universe.

Again,

As from a blazing fire sparks of like substance fly forth a thousandfold, so from the Imperishable, beings manifold are produced, and return thither also.

In the Bhagavad-Gita, Krishna says:

Know the glory of the sun to be mine which illuminates the whole world, and the effulgence of the moon, and the splendor of the fire. I penetrate the clay, and lend all their living force. I glide into the plant . . .

And when the Hindu thinker identifies himself with this One Being in nature he knows himself immortal:

The knowing Self is unborn, It dieth not; eternal, primeval, everlasting. It is not killed, though the body be killed. The slayer thinketh he slayeth; the slain believeth himself destroyed; the thoughts of both are false; the Soul surviveth. It doth not kill, nor doth it die.

This kind of pantheism evidently is not far removed from that of the older writers and romantics we have named.[2] But our newest poets reject it. They disbelieve in the Oversoul and in their own immortality in it, at least in such an idealistic form. Brahman here has too many human qualities projected upon him. Moreover they are too much disabused by experience to read Life or Nature in such optimistic terms. And the new psychology has given them a profound skepticism as to the Self—whether the self of the individual or that of the life force. It is of interest to note that the dissociations produced by modern culture debar men not only from the Jewish-Christian heritage but from the normative and inspiring heritage of India.

Our irrationalist poets are attracted rather by the second strain we have mentioned—the denial of reason and of the human point of view. The Upanishads and the Gita in some aspects insist on the complete otherness of Brahman. Human consciousness must be left behind. Brahman is everything that is not human and not rational. The ecstasy of the Yogin leads at its climax to an experience and a state of which all that can be said is that it is "not

[2] Jung's evidence that the unconscious of modern man testifies to a non-theistic divine power immanent in the Self, together with his appeal to the Upanishads as the clue to the true self or "the complete man," indicates that he roughly classifies the religion of modern western man with this type of pantheism *in its sources*. It is not so realized in its formulation. But Jung also gives plenty of evidence of dissociated moderns whose inner state would assign them rather to the second of our categories.

that!" "not that!" This is nihilism and we get this in some writers today.

What, under correction, appears to be a most striking illustration of this type of naturism, presented with both psychological and poetic power of the first order, is the prose work, *Escapade*, by the distinguished novelist, Evelyn Scott.[3] The book presents a narrative background as follows. The principal character, a woman, who narrates in the first person, has joined a teacher of science who leaves his wife in a certain university town. The university and community ring with scandal which pursues them as they go first to London, then to Rio de Janeiro. The first hopes of securing a living by collecting specimens for a London naturalist have to be abandoned, and John, the lover, has various precarious jobs with commercial agencies. The woman, the narrator, endures the sordid and terrifying cheap hotels. They go from bad to worse financially. Vermin, offensive natives, treacherous servants—and amid all this, pregnancy, childbirth with a mishandled operation and consequent trauma and ill-health, all these breeding in the narrator hatred, bitterness and gall.

[3] The imaginative content of this symbolic novel serves as so good an illustration of our theme in this chapter and introduces so fitly the discussion of Robinson Jeffers that we include it here in a book devoted primarily to poetry. Evelyn Scott was born in Tennessee in the nineties. Her first novels dealt with topics that grow out of family and social tensions in a conventional society. *Escapade* was published in 1923. *The Wave* was the best known of a series of novels presenting historical panoramas of the Civil War and the last half of the nineteenth century. Later volumes, *Eva Gay* and others, are concerned with the artist and his creative problems. Evelyn Scott for all her realism and the trenchancy of her social criticism refuses to be classified with the Marxist writers. She is a moralist in the highest sense as well as an artist. For an account of her work see "Evelyn Scott and Southern Background" by Paula Snelling in *The North Georgia Review*, Vol. II, No. 4 (Winter, 1937-1938).

But the important thing about the book is the quality and intensity of the aesthetic experience that is so conditioned and the beauty of its expression, and especially the insights afforded. The book is a bad dream but a livid and gorgeous one. The narrator speaks of "the gigantic shadows of my delirium." Hysteria has its own sensibility. But to say that this is hysteria is to be ambiguous, for the border lands of hysteria and the artist's imagination are hard to define. What of van Gogh? He would be one to include with our poets, who saw the colors and surfaces of the South with a hyper-sensitivity as of the first man, and erected upon it all a hierarchy of myth and symbolism having the elaborateness of Swedenborg's. The background of Evelyn Scott's book is the South American scene, one used with the power that Lawrence used Mexico. With such a character in such a setting we have pages of hallucination that are a beautiful hallucination. By the aid of her tortured mind she seems to see more vividly the bright forms of life and she goes on to flashes of a philosophy like the nihilism of Jeffers.

Many contemporary painters have this same vision of tropical life and vegetation and color. One would err to suppose that they were merely curious about the exotic forms. Like Evelyn Scott's heroine they see in it a more direct and revealing disclosure of Life itself, whatever it be. And their profoundest quests as artists and as men are tied up with the enigmas they grapple with in such subjects.

It is very curious and significant that the destructive aspects of nature—the typhoon or the rages of the heat or the cholera or the vulture appear to fascinate these artists most deeply and to appear laden with revelation. One finds this everywhere in Jeffers. One finds it in *Escapade*. Speaking of an enormous snake she says: "I enjoy my horror as the whole world falls away from the beautiful shining length of black lacquer and gold, from the symbol of Death which is the name I have given to Nature herself."[4] At other points her imagination is taken with the owl and the hawk.

Surely one is not mistaken in finding a similarity in her view of Nature to Hindu conceptions. Here under a different name is Siva the destroyer—impersonal, unconscious, brilliant beyond all power of expression, imaged by the gorgeous serpent of "black lacquer and gold"—or by the expressionless dancer that goes on in perpetual motion, one posture of beauty succeeding to another. Of life so conceived, terrible and of blinding beauty, we are all a part. Another figure used in the Hindu scriptures for existence in its brilliance but its impersonality is that of the illusory circle of fire made by whirling a blazing brand: "having cut through ignorance he saw Brahman flashing like a wheel on fire, and having seen him he obtained immortality."

In the Upanishads symbols of Brahman are often sought by preference in the nonhuman world. The eagle sloping its wings to sleep in motion, the spider that goes out of itself by means of its thread, the serpent and that serpent of the heavens—the lightning, all these appear. For "that art Thou":

The dark-blue bird, and the green parrot with red eyes;
Thou hast the lightning as thy child;
Thou art the seasons and the seas.

4 P. 206.

Often the sense is primarily that Brahman is all things or the source of all things. But his impersonal and numinous quality is brought into the foreground by the symbols used.

Among serpents I am the symbol of eternity. I am the circumference of the waters, the grandsire among the Fathers, and in the measurement of days, lo, I am Death.[5]

In the Gita Krishna and Arjuna converse of the alternative pathways to realization. One can worship the divine manifestation in visible things, centering one's thought on the Self and devoting one's self to the personal Krishna. But a greater travail is to seek "the Unperceived and Indestructible":

Yet their travail is the greater, for the attainment of God unmanifested is a goal very difficult for the soul in human body to reach.[6]

It is this more difficult goal that is touched in *Escapade*.

We find, moreover, in Evelyn Scott's book as in other contemporaries the answer of much Hindu thought. Salvation for us is to be disabused of our individuality, our "masquerade in differentness," as the narrator calls it. "We must get rid of all we know, go back. Feed ourselves to Nature who is greater than Moloch."[7] The following quotations bear on her conception of the deeper being, in nature. ". . . true being is behind and beyond words. Awareness is altogether fragmentary and derived . . ."

[5] *The Song of God* (Translation of the Bhagavad-Gita), by D. G. Mukerji, p. 95.
[6] *Ibid.*, pp. 112-113.
[7] P. 223.

"Evening. On the virginal mountain there is a glow like the blooming of heavenly hyacinths in a dark, dark field. My own warmth goes out of me with the light. I am as cold as the shadows, I am chill denial, chaos again, the unnamed thing."[8]

"The unnamed thing" is her name for life. She uses violent expressions to make it clearer to herself, expressions calculated to convey its alienness, its mystery, its blankness; the most graphic of which is that of the sightless fetus. This idea recurs in many forms. "Consumed by life, our eyes are closed in the undreamt belly of the night."[9] What she is affirming is that our true existence and our true oneness with life is something deeper than our rational consciousness; deeper than our human individuality—ultimately deeper than our human nature itself. She feels Life as a tremendous Force—fascinating in its infinite forms and shows and prodigious in its amoral power. Our true existence, "our unstated being," however, is not among the forms and shows but in identity with the unknowable power, the unnamed thing. Evidently the clues to this Power, the symbols of true existence, that is, will be found apart from the sympathetic aspects of nature. This is not pantheism as we usually know it but nihilism.

Those who know Evelyn Scott's later work know that she is at home in quite contrary points of view.[10] It is indeed rare that an occidental should recreate and relive the experiences of ancient India, or rather spontaneously discover them for himself. If our view is correct it is possible in the conditions of modern culture where one

[8] Pp. 204, 218.
[9] P. 218.
[10] See pp. 176, 177.

sensitively bearing its maladies is suddenly thrown into the tropics or some region equally favorable. The instance of Keyserling could be added.[11] Such a rediscovery of primitivism, is, however, not to be recommended. Its first condition is the instability of the personal consciousness, the ruling feature of our time, a form and degree of dissociation that lend a pronounced unreality to life, thus encouraging all degrees of pantheism and monism. The end of the road in such experience appears to be a reversion to sub-personal forms of faith or primitivism in the sinister sense. Those who would escape from the stifling air of our civilization should go forward rather than back. We should create habitable oases of wholesomeness and organic living in the midst of our modern cities by the renewal of our great religious traditions.

[11] Compare also, Wallace Stevens' poem, "The Comedian as the Letter C," in the section, "II: Concerning the Thunderstorms of Yucatan," in *Harmonium*, 1923.

CHAPTER XII

THE NIHILISM OF MR. ROBINSON JEFFERS

The satisfaction that men take in evidences of the life of nature and especially in its power, and above all in surpassing manifestations of that power, is one of the perennial roots of religion. If it has been the ground of world-wide primitive religion, or one of its grounds, we may be sure that it reappears today among sophisticated minds. And this especially where such minds turn from habits of intellectualism or mechanism to rediscover vital moods. Such a trend has been marked in contemporary art in some quarters.

The following citation gives an eloquent description of the effects on the mind of one of the most prodigious of nature's manifestations, and will serve to illuminate this trend in the new poetry. It is taken from a monograph on Vesuvius by a student of volcanic phenomena, Dr. Frank A. Perret.[1]

Strongest of all impressions received in the course of these remarkable events, greatest of all surprises . . . was, for the writer, that of an infinite dignity in every manifestation of this stupendous releasing of energy. No words can describe the majesty of its unfolding, the utter absence of anything resembling effort, and the all-sufficient power to perform the allotted task and to do it majestically. Each rapid impulse was the

[1] *The Vesuvius Eruption of 1906; Study of a Volcanic Cycle* (Washington, D. C., The Carnegie Institution, 1924), pp. 46, 47.

crest of something deep and powerful and uniform which bore it, and the unhurried modulation of its rhythmic beats sets this eruption in the rank of things which are mighty, grave and great.

There was present also the element of awe, in all its fullness. The phenomena entered, through their intensity, that sphere where the normal conditions of Nature are overpassed, and one stands in the presence of greater and more elemental forces than any he has known hitherto. This tends to induce a state of mind which hardly recognizes as entirely natural this transformation of the visible universe, and with difficulty one accepts the dictum of reason, that all will pass and the normal return as before; and so, for the many, the events of this and the succeeding days of ashy darkness seemed to show that— even as the younger Pliny wrote of similar conditions in this same region nearly two thousand years ago—"the last eternal night of story has settled on the world."

But it is precisely this projection beyond the borderland of the obvious which gives to such events their majesty—the dignity which, allied with the mysterious, is thereby perfected. The sense-walls of the Universe are shattered by these higher values of power, and Deity is indirectly more in evidence than in the case of lesser things. A blade of grass as surely, but far less forcibly, reveals the truth that That which manifests cannot be seen, nor heard, nor felt, except through and because of the manifestation.

It is some such sense of the greater and more elemental forces of nature which supplies one of the most powerful attractions in the work of Robinson Jeffers. Volcanoes offer these manifestations only occasionally, but for the unjaded eye the mountains and the sea are constantly to be found "in the rank of things which are mighty, grave and great." "The sense walls of the Universe are shattered by these higher values of power, and Deity is indirectly more in evidence than in the case of lesser things." Mr. Jeffers would not ordinarily use the concept of Deity though he can on occasion, but it is in the elemental and untamed in nature that he finds the clues of salvation, of what lies behind and before the human consciousness.

Here, then, he rejoins the tendency we have found in *Escapade* and in one strain of the Upanishads, to seek out and beyond the human for a solution, and to find the symbols for this in those apparitions of nature that are most alien. When the narrator in *Escapade* bid us "get rid of all we know, go back. Feed ourselves to Nature," so we read in Jeffers, "Return through the original fountain." One may not speak finally about any particular credo of this poet. There is occasional contradiction of his themes, but the ones we stress will be found to recur.

Apart from the lyrics the work of Jeffers consists of narrative poems of some length written in a Whitmanesque line presenting dramas or rather melodramas of more than usually violent and repellent character. Often the characterization and action is cloudily presented and the style loose, but in the best poems, *Roan Stallion, The Tower Beyond Tragedy, Cawdor, Give Your Heart to the Hawks,* these become sharper and more powerful, and one recognizes in any case that the poems are not to be judged first of all as narratives. Mr. Yvor Winters has been severe upon deficiencies both literary and psychological of the stories. If there is a moral equivalence about all actions, he protests, we are deprived of what is indispensable, for dramatic and human interest. This alleged moral indifference plus the nihilistic philosophy results in a condition of being "numb to the intricacies of human feeling" and how can dramatic narrative poetry excel with these limitations? ". . . it remains again a fair question whether a moral monist *can* arrive at any clear conclusions about the value of a course of action, since he denies the existence of any conceivable standard of values within the strict limits of human life as such." Mr. Winters' criticism is telling but some of Jeffers' material eludes the charges. The point is that these poems ordinarily should not be read or judged by the canons of narrative. They are hymns of salvation, and the dramatic interest lies not in any cogent sequence of human interest (though in *Give Your Heart to the Hawks* such sequence is felt) but in the constant tension between the life of man and the goal beyond it.

Thus with regard to *The Tower Beyond Tragedy*, which treats of the crime of Orestes, Winters says: "But at the very last moment, in Mr. Jeffers' version, Orestes is converted to Mr. Jeffers' religion and goes off explaining . . . that though men may think he is fleeing before the furies he is really drifting up to the mountains to meditate on the stars; and the preceding action is, of course, rendered morally and emotionally meaningless." It is not rendered morally meaningless, because Jeffers' interest is to throw the light upon the way men torment themselves with duty and scruple and conscience, and this is the more effective here by contrast with Orestes' present enlightenment. It is not emotionally meaningless because it is by contrast with those passions and torments now known to be neutral and inconsequential that the solution is realized.

The literary interest of the poems is comparatively minor. It comes out occasionally in the eloquent passages on nature or comparing nature and man, or in the occa-

sional lyric philosophy, or in the powerful utterances of
remorse and alienation. But the chief interest of the work
is its philosophical attitude and for this purpose much is
of interest which is poor literature. The case is much the
same with D. H. Lawrence, not to say Walt Whitman,
though the credos are different. The question is asked,
Why should a person with an allegedly "normal" view of
life be interested in the view presented by Jeffers? The
only answer can be that whole races of men have thought
and felt similarly, that many of our own time undoubtedly
have hauntings of this kind, and that nothing human is
alien to us. Moreover if we would change such a world
view we must understand it.

The reason for the repellent themes of crime and incest
is found stated in a passage from *Roan Stallion*. It is indicated that revelation and clues of the superman come
not from the usual and conventional experiences but from
the exceptional and rebellious. We are reminded of Rimbaud's search for illumination, and can recognize a kind
of travesty of the myth of Prometheus or the doctrine of
the Cross:

> Humanity is
> the start of the race; I say
> Humanity is the mold to break away from, the crust to break
> through, the coal to break into fire,
> The atom to be split.
> Tragedy that breaks man's face and a white fire flies out
> of it; vision that fools him
> Out of his limits, desire that fools him out of his limits,
> unnatural crime, inhuman science . . .
> These break, these pierce, these deify.

The theme is that man has a best chance often to be stung awake by experiences that force him beyond himself. To create situations that present this kind of possibility Jeffers recurs to the drastic experiences of unnatural crime, incest or matricide, and to their consequences of remorse and the struggle with remorse. Only so does he come to the frontiers of the nonhuman, realizing the insignificance of man, reason, conscience and law. He apparently has an acute sense of the horrible sufferings that can be occasioned by blame, by the sense of guilt, and he would relieve men of that.

> Oh, ignorant penitents,
> For surely the cause is too small for so much anguish.
> To be drunk is a folly, to kill may call judgment down,
> But these are not enormous evils.[2]

Jeffers gets his sense of the comparative inconsequence of man particularly from the contrast with nature to which we have referred. Living in his stone tower over Monterey Bay he has before him the Pacific Ocean, on which, as he says, a thousand-mile hurricane is only a shadow. About him are the crags of the shore and behind him the austere granite ranges.

> On account of the dull weather
> And closing twilight the group on the hill top was hardly
>   visible in the vast scene. It was quite evident
> That not only Pico Blanco against the north, and the grey
>   Ventanas, but even every dry fold
> And gully of the humbler hills was almost by an infinite meas-
>   ure of more importance
> Than the few faint figures on the bare heights.[3]

[2] *Give Your Heart to the Hawks*, p. 27.
[3] *Ibid.*, pp. 35, 36.

But men are not only insignificant, they are corrupt. Despite the occasions when a doctrine of moral equivalence appears to be taught, those that argue original sin will find their testimony here as in other of the new poets. The human heart is vile, the human mind is a spider weaving treacheries. Man has corrupted himself in his societies, in his taboos and in his laws. He would echo the lines of Aiken,

> O Man, who so corrupt all things you feed on;
> Whose meditation slimes the thing it thinks;
> Vile borer into the core of the universe;
> Spoiler and destroyer. ("Poverty Grass")

Thus for every reason death or the discovery of the sense of death in nature is to be desired. It is to life as "heaven over deep hell." Who once being dead would rise again?

Resurrection to join this midge-dance
Of gutted and multiplied echoes of life in the latter sun?
Dead man be quiet. A fool of a merchant, who'd sell good earth
And grass again to make modern flesh. ("No Resurrection")

The positive teaching of Jeffers offers an escape for man from this condition into a nihilist Nirvana—a return through the original fountain. Nature is only a symbol for that which is not consciousness, not mind, not man. We are again on the ground of the Upanishads in the aspect described. The Sierras and the stars and prehistoric cromlechs of Ireland and the life of the eagle have signified to him that there is an "unstated being" in the universe that is everything that man is not.

That such a quest is not something that can be set aside as peculiar and special is suggested by discovering it again in Mr. J. C. Powys, in *A Philosophy of Solitude*. We are "harassed megalopolitans," he says. There is no help for us in the romantic philosophies of Emerson, Whitman and their kind. We must find our salvation by "sinking down into the mystery of the inanimate." We are to be planetary elementalists. To quote a review of the book by Mr. Alfred Schmalz, "Our salvation . . . is in becoming 'elementalists,' that is, 'lovers of the Inanimate.' This does not mean that we are to become lovers of nature, for nature is too self-assertive, too full of 'struggling, contending, teeming lives'—the very thing we must escape. Rather, being selective in our appreciations, we ought to establish an intimate relation to nature in her starkest, barest, most simple aspects; in short with the cosmic elements—earth, stone, rock, water, air, vapor."[4] Mr. Powys invokes the names of Epictetus, Marcus Aurelius and Lao-tzu. But other names, Wordsworth, Rousseau, are added, and the eclecticism and occasional bathos serve to discredit the doctrine. Evidently there is no remote promontory or archipelago of speculation or phantasy about which men of our time are not to be seen clambering or pushing their frail craft. "You do not see that the Real is in your home, and you wander from forest to forest listlessly," said Kabir.

Jeffers' conception is represented very often in terms of the life of wild creatures as well as of inanimate nature. There is the same particular attention here to the eagle, the owl, the jackal, the snake, that we see in *Escapade*. The mystery of life is often felt with peculiar force in these

[4] *The Christian Century*, Dec. 6, 1933.

creatures that live, but that live in ways so alien to men and often so independently of men. This thought is stressed in the speech of God in the climax of the Book of Job, to bring home to him that "the Eternal hath his own purposes" and that existence has other concerns than human. Of course in the Book of Job important complementary attributes of Deity are assumed which give a totally different final picture of him.

But Jeffers not only recurs again and again to these creatures; he seems to have a perverse interest in showing them under torture. A deer caught in barbed wire, a rabbit aflame from the prairie fire, lobsters cooking alive, a wounded Cooper's hawk fighting a gamecock to death, a coyote caught in two steel traps at once so that it cannot stand or lie, a yearling colt swollen with the sting of a rattler—we are apt to say masochism or sadism and satisfy ourselves with that. There is probably no one writing today that is so cruel, with the possible exception of Faulkner. But Jeffers is at least consistent. For his conception of life is of a prodigiously beautiful force that makes its way through shining and splendid creations (man apart), but bleeds as it goes. This will be illustrated by a passage from *Cawdor*. The captive eagle which is the symbol and clue of the whole drama has been blinded and killed, and the passage tells of the vision of the phantom as it soars higher and higher:

It saw, according to the sight of its kind, the archetype
Body of life a beaked carnivorous desire
Self-upheld on storm-broad wings: but the eyes
Were spouts of blood; the eyes were gashed out; dark blood
Ran from the ruinous eye-pits to the hook of the beak

And rained on the waste spaces of empty heaven.
Yet the great Life continued; yet the great Life
Was beautiful, and she drank her defeat, and devoured
Her famine for food.
                            There the eagle's phantom perceived
Its prison and its wound were not its peculiar wretchedness,
All that lives was maimed and bleeding, caged or in blindness,
Lopped at the ends with death and conception, and shrewd
Cautery of pain on the stumps to stifle the blood, but not
Refrains for all that; life was more than its functions
And accidents, more important than its pains and pleasures,
A torch to burn in with pride, a necessary
Ecstasy in the run of the cold substance,
And scape-goat of the greater world. (But as for me,
I have heard the summer dust crying to be born
As much as ever flesh cried to be quiet.)
Pouring itself on fulfilment the eagle's passion
Left life behind and flew at the sun, its father.
The great unreal talons took peace for prey
Exultantly, their death beyond death; stooped upward, and
        struck
Peace like a white fawn in a dell of fire.[5]

Here there is an affirmation of life both in its empirical
aspect and in that peace, that death beyond death, which
it finds when it leaves "life" behind. But the appreciation
of life in its empirical aspect is amoral and aesthetic. So
he can speak in "Still the Mind Smiles" of knowing, that
all evils remain

Beautiful in the whole fabric, excesses that balance each other
Like the paired wings of a flying bird.

  [5] Compare the following lines from the eighth chapter of the Bhagavad-
Gita (Mukerji's translation): "thus shalt the soul by steadfast devotion
hold the conception of My being within the unstable mind, *and pierce
hawk-like beyond death, into my transcendent radiance.*"

Misery and riches, civilization and squalid savagery,
Mass war and the odor of unmanly peace . . .[6]

It is never safe to pin this writer down to a given sentiment as is so unjustly done. His poems evidence often an ethical activity which clashes with this last citation. But it can be concluded that there is a disgust with man and an exaltation of that which is beyond life which leaves him numb to the intricacies of human feeling," which as Winters says is a limitation of all mystical poetry. The person who is concerned with ethical and personal values will query as to the conditions that lead our contemporaries to such misanthropy. It has been pointed out that a certain type of romantic primitivism akin to that we find here, essentially subjective, despite its avowed concern with nature, acts to blind the artist from all but the irrational forces of his own soul. Such a condition finds an eastern nihilism a welcome framework into which to cast its introspective ecstasies. The work of Jeffers is not to be classed with the solipsistic irrationalism of such a poet as Crane, however. We have here too evidently a notable objectivity toward the majesty of nature. Thus the reproach against a certain type of elementalist made by Winters is not fully pertinent here, that he is "interested in getting just as far off in the direction of the uncontrolled, the meaningless, as he can possibly get and still have the pleasure of talking about it . . . he would if he could

[6] The de-personalizing of the individual by whatever method leads in the direction of a doctrine of moral equivalence. At times, but only at times, we feel that the method with Mr. Jeffers is the same as that in the following passage from the Chandogya Upanishad: "Once the Self knows this, 'I am that'—it is harmed by no deed whatsoever, neither by theft, nor by slaying the babe unborn, nor by slaying his mother, or his father. Nor when he has done evil deeds does the bloom leave his face."

devote himself to exploring that realm of experience which he shares with sea-anemones, cabbages and onions, in preference to the realm of experience shared specifically with men." If one must deprecate Mr. Jeffers one will say that he leans too much toward Nietzsche, rather than that he leans toward the totemist!

CHAPTER XIII

THE PRIMITIVISM OF D. H. LAWRENCE

The feeling about nature of D. H. Lawrence is less strange to us than that of the last two writers we have considered. It is the feeling of one who has awarenesses and sympathies that go far beyond those of the ordinary man, but it is the more usually beloved and familiar aspects of nature that he delights in, despite his roamings to Mexico and Sardinia. What drew him to these lands was not the quest for an inhuman nature, but for a primitive setting where man and beast and bird, village and mountain lived together unharassed by civilization. There are religious elements in Lawrence's feeling for nature, but they fall under the head of pantheism rather than nihilism. Lawrence was willing to surrender the intellect of man, but not the blood; the cerebral but not the vegetal and sensuous. Thus he is not in company with the complete rejection of the human by Jeffers.

It is true that he loathed the life of man in civilized society, and he could, like Jeffers, show the insignificance of man over against nature. Speaking of snowy hills in an English winter he writes,

From the height it is very beautiful. The upland is naked, white like silver, and moving far into the distance, strange and muscular, with gleams like skin. Only the wind surprises one, invisibly cold; the sun lies bright on a field, like the movement of a sleeper. It is strange how insignificant in all this life seems. Two men, tiny as dots, move from a farm on a snow slope, carrying hay to the beasts. Every moment they seem to melt like insignificant spots of dust; the sheer, living, muscular white of the uplands absorbs everything. Only there is a tiny clump of trees bare on the hill-top—small beeches—writhing like iron in the blue sky.—I wish one could cease to be a human being, and be a demon. Allzu menschlich.[1]

Lawrence thus, like the nihilists, could even wish to cease to be a human being, as in the conclusion of the passage. He could, as so commonly in the literature of mysticism, use the metaphor of death and extinction as a symbol of deliverance.

> if I could lift my feet,
> My tenacious feet, from off the dome of the earth
> To fall like a breath within the breathing wind
> Where you are lost, what rest, my love, what rest![2]

He could express a revulsion against human nature as tainted with the flesh[3] or with self:

> I was so weary with the world,
> I was so sick of it,
> everything was tainted with myself,
> skies, trees, flowers, birds, water,
> people, houses, streets, vehicles, machines,
> nations, armies, war, peace-talking,
> work, recreation, governing, anarchy,
> it was all tainted with myself, I knew it all to start with
> because it was all myself.[4]

---

[1] *The Letters of D. H. Lawrence* (New York, 1932), p. 473.
[2] *Collected Poems* (1932), "Call Into Death," p. 169.
[3] *Ibid.*, "Craving for Spring," pp. 345, 346.
[4] *Ibid.*, p. 325.

So he would desire to die, and yet always as here antici-
pating the resurrected self from the wellheads of the new
world:

> The unknown, strong current of life supreme
> drowns me and sweeps me away and holds me down
> to the sources of mystery, in the depths,
> extinguishes there my risen resurrected life
> and kindles it further at the core of utter mystery.[5]

He can use the term God to state the same theme in one of
his later poems:

> then I must know that still
> I am in the hands of the unknown God,
> he is breaking me down to his own oblivion
> to send me forth on a new morning, a new man.[6]

Lawrence is unique among contemporary heretics and
disbelievers in his insistence on the resurrection, the resurrection of the body. It is an aspect of his anti-spirituality
and anti-Platonism, and his affirmation of the senses as
the true mediators of the eternal mystery. Jeffers, we
would say, does affirm some continuing ecstasy in his
Nirvana, but it is a dehumanized ecstasy. Lawrence does
not thus disconnect the present and the ultimate experience. If it is true to say that "that which I wish to be, that
in some sense I am," we may say that Lawrence *was*,
indeed, what he expressed the wish to be, a demon and not
a man, but he was a human demon. His uncanny "em-
pathy" for the forms of nature was the gift of a demon,

[5] *Ibid.*, pp. 329, 330.
[6] From *Last Poems*, "Shadows," p. 78.

one that slips in and out of the trunks of trees, that has the freedom of all the precincts of the earth and sea, a familiar of sun, moon, and stars, dawn and midnight, and that runs with fox and weasel. But he was a human demon because he could pass through walls and doors in all that concerned human secrets, and could explore and bring back intelligence of the soul and flesh of the human, both man and woman, no less than of other wild creatures.

What philosophy he gives expression to is a rather undistinguished merger of pantheism and Bergsonism. We see the anti-intellectualism,

Then perhaps in the dark you'd get what you want to find:
The solution that ever is much too deep for mind;
    Dissolved in the blood . . .[7]

"My great religion is a belief in the blood, the flesh, as being wiser than the intellect. We can go wrong in our minds. But what our blood feels, and believes, and says, is always true."[8] And the common garden variety of pantheism is expressed in the following unexciting way:

For now I know
The world within worlds is a womb, whence issues all
The shapeliness that decks us here—below:
And the same fire that boils within this ball
Of earth, and quickens all herself with flowers,
Is womb-fire in the stiffened clay of us.

Lawrence insisted that he was "a passionately religious man." "There is a *principle* in this universe, toward which

[7] *Collected Poems*, p. 145, "These Clever Women."
[8] Cited by A. Huxley, Introduction to *Letters* . . . p. xiv.

man turns religiously—a *life* of the universe itself. And the hero is he who touches and transmutes the life of the universe." Huxley stresses how he was possessed by his creative genius, citing the passage. "I often think one ought to be able to pray before one works—and then leave it to the Lord . . . I always feel as though I stood naked for the fire of Almighty God to go through me—and it's rather an awful feeling. One has to be so terribly religious, to be an artist." He was indeed so religious in his understanding of his poetry that he looked on it as oracular rather than artistic and was little inclined to revise it. Of a very different type of poet we have much the same thing said. Darrell Figgis says of Æ: "Many of his poems come not only from the inmost circle of spiritual insight, but also from the outer circle of psychic vision; and much that might seem, at a cursory glance, extravagant imagery, will be found to be no more than meticulous accuracy to what he has beheld . . . And there are many poems of this sort, that are rather less poems than texts, like the texts of the East, to be brooded upon like symbols and unravelled like mysteries . . . For this poet conceived highly of Life, and conceived highly of Poetry, the first and purest handmaiden of Life."[9]

Thus both were extreme romantics about their poetry, romantics *enragés*. Where Lawrence wrote with his body, Æ wrote with his "soul." Passable poetry in either case only issued when either by some accident involved the imagination in his work. Æ had the good judgment to shape his work a little. Lawrence's religion or intoxication was of a kind more calculated to appeal to his generation

[9] *Æ* (*George W. Russell*) (New York, 1917), p. 41.

so that it is adjudged better literature. As a matter of fact it is probably the man that makes the appeal, and the novelist, not the poet. But Lawrence the prophet finds expression in his poetry.

The aspect of Lawrence that has won him his influence and made him a legend is the good show he put up of being the only man *alive* in an empty, diseased, and mechanized world. He set up a cult of those who could say, "we are the living," and who could commiserate or scorn infected mass men, "the *filthy* world," the canaille, and who must necessarily confine their tolerance for humanity to a few individuals. "I've had enough of the social passion . . . I'm out on a new track—let humanity go its own way—I go mine." Like Whitman, he gave the impression of a magnificent spontaneity and enfranchisement. In some men the sheer gifts of nature are poured in such volume that in their presence all other values except vitality are confounded, any true scrutiny of good and bad, right and wrong, is dazzled. The miracle of life is felt for what it is in the inexhaustible freshness of nature, only it is felt the more miraculously because it comes mediated through a human being. Such men make disciples, though neither master nor disciple is able in the powerful distraction of sheer talent to distinguish truth from falsehood. "To be with Lawrence," says Huxley, "was a kind of adventure, a voyage of discovery into newness and otherness. For, being himself of a different order, he inhabited a different universe from that of common men . . ."[10]

[10] See also Knud Merrild, *A Poet and Two Painters, A Memoir of D. H. Lawrence* (London, 1938), pp. 87, 88: "He evoked new rhythms, sleeping energies, and cleared one's vision . . . He made one conscious of a new awareness . . . One was still the same, but life within and without pulsated more quickly, more colourfully and in a clearer light!"

His special genius was his ability to see life with the freshness of a convalescent, and to penetrate familiarly the penumbra of mystery and darkness in all life and forms, those zones and levels in which so much of deeper reality lies hidden. And all this he could report. It was by a gift of intuitive sympathy that he could do this. He seemed to be free from the stultification which civilized man suffers from his intellect and his conventionalism. With him the organic bond with nature had not been severed. Thus he had a freshness of perception and spontaneity of person which sharply rebuked his age, and made him seem uniquely alive. His protest against the machine, against the strangulation of men by devitalized moral and social convention, his plea for life, his denunciation of a bloodless spirituality, his Bergsonian irrationalism, all these made him a prophet to a time afflicted as we have seen the time to be.

From his gospel of spontaneity and his anti-spirituality or "mystical materialism" we may anticipate his ethics. It has been misjudged especially in the area of the sexes. The true authority for conduct, he would say, is inspiration. This does not mean sheer arbitrary impulse, for Lawrence recognized that "a man should *never* do the thing he believes to be wrong. Because if he does, he loses his own singleness, wholeness, natural honour."[11] But a man's conduct should be deeply directed by inspiration. That is, morality is an art, a very personal and creative art, into which enter as in any art the given materials and the creative impulse. The given materials are the proper determinants of the form it shall take, not some external

[11] Merrild, *op. cit.*, p. 234.

pattern. He had a strong conviction of the God within him, and to this power or powers he looked for the deepest fulfillment of existence. He could call him his own "Holy Ghost." He more usually spoke of it in the plural. "For me, there are also many gods, that come into me and leave me again. And they have their various wills, I must say."[12] Whatever these gods prompted with their blinding control won Lawrence's assent and this sanctioned his conduct. He trusted his numen. It might be an impulse of anger. It might be a dark god or a bright one.

"Lawrence said: I believe:

"That I am I.

"That my soul is a dark forest.

"That my known self will never be more than a little clearing in the forest.

"That gods, strange gods, come forth from the forest into the clearing of my known self, and then go back.

"That I must have the courage to let them come and go.

"That I will never let mankind put anything over on me, but that I will try always to recognize and submit to the gods in me and the gods in other men and women . . ."[13]

The reader of Lawrence's letters, poems and conversations soon concludes that he had no very clear code and that he contradicted himself often. His personal qualities as a man belied much of the seeming antinomianism of his teaching. On the other hand there is no doubt that his essential philosophy of life was an uncritical dependence on the irrational. With his insistence as to the sacred in the instinctive life he could give no adequate guidance for

[12] *Ibid.*, p. 235.
[13] Merrild, *op. cit.*, p. 238.

the important discriminations that necessarily should have been added.

Yet it is not just to call Lawrence immoral or amoral. He assigned a very solemn sense of significance and sacredness to the Mystery from which his experiences came, and indicated as *immoral* whatever frustrated or blasphemed against it. Thus life surrendered to or involved in abstractions, in duties that were merely scruples and habits and not alive, or to idealisms that were anemic and that left the person and the body emaciated and mutilated; all such he viewed as immoral just as William Blake did in his way. Moreover, to the area of the sexes Lawrence assigned a sacredness many of his mistaken followers have ignored, and he could be profoundly shocked by frivolity or commercialism or calculated hedonism in these matters. He was no doubt profoundly at sea in his philosophy of these and other ethical matters, but it is important to understand the ground of the protest he made, as with Blake and Whitman. A society that stunts and smothers the natural life of man, in the name of religion or out of a long tradition of inhibition and restraint or in mechanized and artificial modes of life is bound to see recurrent figures protesting in the name of some form of primitivism or naturalism. The message of Lawrence is understood in the light of the culture we have described in our earlier chapters.

It is of interest, at this point, to test Lawrence by the factors we have earlier presented to see how far his own outlook was influenced by modern conditions making for negation or disarray. His particular gift for the apprehension of nature and his freedom from sophistication

saved him from many of the ills that afflicted the Waste
Land school. He lived in organic unity with nature, and
neither immediate war experience nor absorption with the
new psychology or prolonged megalopolitan residence
were factors in his case. He did, however, suffer long and
acutely as a young man from frustration of the sexual life
consequent upon Anglo-Saxon attitudes, as is evident
from *Sons and Lovers.* The account of the interminable,
hesitant and inhibited courtship is generally understood
to be autobiographical.

More particularly, however, Lawrence was a victim of
the third disorganization in modern life we have listed—
that is the broken social tie between the individual and
the group. Lawrence was an agonized solitary, sometimes
drawn to isolation, but again powerfully drawn toward a
social connection he was unable long to sustain. This no
doubt grew in large part out of his gift. It is part of the
problem of the artist at all times, one to which Thomas
Mann, for instance, has continually recurred. The artist
is neither fish nor fowl; an Ishmaelite in the earth. But
more than that, the particular acuteness of the problem
for Lawrence grew out of the nature of our society, of his
British society in war and between wars, where the salient
individual was inevitably without a "tribe," without a context. It appears in one aspect in the fantastic insecurity in
which he lived. In a very revealing letter to a psychologist
he says, "What ails me is the absolute frustration of my
primeval societal instinct . . . I think societal instinct
much deeper than sex instinct—and societal repression
much more devastating. There is no repression of the
sexual individual comparable to the repression of the

societal man in me, by the individual ego, my own and everybody else's . . . Myself, I suffer badly from being so cut off . . ."[14]

In another letter Lawrence blames the world, in this case, the war, for his separateness: "the *oneness* of mankind is destroyed in me." Thus, though he had the companionship and love of his wife, Frieda, he was uprooted and torn out of society. (Behind the whole story is the home he grew up in with the poignant scenes of the colliery worker's family in Nottinghamshire which we can recover from his greatest novel.) Such a social situation undoubtedly had a part to play in the sadness of his later days and in the fact that his views of life and conduct never met corrective experience. It is true that within the limits of his mode of life he lived out his views to the great cost of himself and his wife, but our errors are never so drastically brought home to us as when we are obliged to live in wide responsible relations.

But whether the nihilism of Jeffers or the ethical fallacies of D. H. Lawrence, all such doctrines are only part of a general anti-Christian and anti-Jewish wave of heresy, a neopaganism appearing in many forms. Marx and Nietzsche are the two most significant names connected with it, but the general hostility to the Hebrew-Christian view of life is conditioned by much more than the influence of individuals. The indifference toward Christianity of a Valéry, the modern stoicism of an E. A. Robinson, the philosophy of recurrences of an O'Neill or a Pound, the Celtic paganism of a Yeats, the blasphemy of a Lawrence,

[14] Letter to Dr. T. Burrow, cited in Huxley's Introduction, pp. xxii, xxiii, *op. cit.*

these and many more go back to a deep dilemma of our culture as to values. The issues between paganism and Christianity have not been clear. Christianity has allowed a major ambiguity to remain unsolved in the eyes of generations, of which advantage has been taken by man's "unchristened heart." That ambiguity concerns the affirmation of life. The Christian has not made clear for himself the paradox of world denial and abundance of life. He has lodged in an otherworldliness that has seemed, whether to a Nietzsche or a Lawrence, a blasphemy against the natural creation, or in a compromise with life that has lost any creative appeal, and so deserved the apostasy of those thirsty for reality.

"When I began to dig into the arguments which modern man makes against Christianity, and especially to investigate militant atheism in the U. S. S. R.," says Berdyaev, "I came to the conclusion that there was one chief argument, one main reason for estrangement from Christianity and hostility to the faith. People of modern civilization who are inclined to be anti-Christian always say one thing, always present the chief argument: the Christian religion lowers man, rejects his activity and creativeness, teaches him to lay everything on God and on the grace which proceeds from God. Man is called to humility and obedience, he must humble himself before evil, darkness and injustice. Man is considered a sinful, fallen being, that is, incapable of building up a better life and unworthy of a better life. Thus Christianity appears as a religion of slaves." And again, "But to modern man, deaf to the mystical side of Christianity, the Christian faith seems a compromise with evil and suffering, humility before injustice, a refusal to struggle. In this way the two hostile arguments against Christianity are joined together. If man freed himself from faith in God, he could at any rate freely struggle with his human activity against evil, suffering and injustice, and if he did not destroy them, he might diminish them, reduce them to the minimum."[15]

Orthodox religion will then have to set its own house in order if it is to obviate the bitter nihilism we meet in Jeffers or the destructive primitivism of D. H. Lawrence. It must show itself an asset rather than a liability in man's struggle against social inertia; but more fundamentally it must clarify its true doctrine of original sin so as not to inhibit the affirmation of life, including the affirmation of the body. It is true that natural man will always find in Christianity a certain ascetic claim. All natural goods must be tested not only by consideration of the whole of society but also by the Christian norms for self-fulfillment. A price must be paid for the common life. Individualism even its more splendid forms not only mars community but plunges into unreality and madness. Nevertheless, the primordial gifts of life are to be reverenced, utilized and exalted, as some individualists like Nietzsche and Lawrence have been obliged to insist. It will be the task of high religion in the future to show how the spiritual goals it pursues can include and require all human gifts that make for abundance of life.

[15] "Grounds for Hostility to Christianity," in *The Student World*, Geneva, Switzerland, Vol. XXXI, No. 2 (Second Quarter, 1938), pp. 107, 108.

CHAPTER XIV

ETHICAL MOTIVES

There is much to be said for the thesis that the most significant and searching discussion of ethics today is going on not in the churches but outside them. The post-war or between-war generation was precipitated into dilemmas of such acuteness both in the personal and in the social area that it has had to shape an empiricist ethics in the face of actual experience. Such trial and error conclusions as it has reached are not, after all, completely improvised. The experience of the past has been present as an implicit factor even where supposedly disregarded. As a result notable affirmations of value and designs of living have been struck off without benefit at least of contemporary clergy, though their sponsors might be discomfited to realize what an array of saints and churchmen of old stand behind their assumptions. Not least would this be true of the communist poets, but it would also be true of other schools of poetry, primitivist or pagan, at points where they are moved by moral indignation, nostalgia for greater days, and impulses toward fuller realization. If we are to look today for the areas where true ethical passion is most alive and where the issues of conduct and social obligation are most poignantly mooted it will be in certain growing edges of the churches, but especially in the secular and agnostic literature of today, particularly in fiction.

There is a general tendency on the part of the orthodox and the fastidious to deplore twentieth-century realist fiction. It presents large slices of contemporary paganism. The writings of Dreiser, Sherwood Anderson, Hemingway, Dos Passos, Faulkner, Farrell do, indeed, raise those most baffling questions that have to do with the proper sphere of art and the proper handling of its material. It is possible, however, for one who pretends to judge such material, whether in fiction or in poetry, from a Christian point of view to defend the writers.[1] Too often the traditionalist in his attacks on O'Neill or Caldwell or Eliot gives the case away by making it clear that what he really likes and likes alone is Hugh Walpole, Priestley, the *Mutiny on the Bounty* and good historical and regional romance. This latter literature we may agree is wholesome, but it is not whole. It is not in this field as a rule that we find the crucial issues of contemporary life dealt with. Such issues have an ugly side, and the art that deals with them may well be ugly. Thoughtful contemporary readers are often tired of reading stories, even good ones. They are tired of some types of brave souls that for all their courage have no curiosities, and they are tired of certain giants in the earth that have no subtlety, and in general of stories and story writers that do not seem to know that the molds are broken today, not only the outer patterns but the deeper molds. They want psychology and sociology in their fiction, and unhackneyed ethical issues; not in doses, indeed, but in the warp and woof of it. And they want literature that deals with the front line today, where salvation and damnation are going on, even if some of the wit-

[1] For a judicious discussion of these matters see H. E. Luccock, *Contemporary American Literature and Religion* (Chicago, 1934).

nesses are among the damned. They are not content to have it in social surveys and criminal statistics. They want it in fiction.

A recent review of a book by O'Flaherty says: "Such a book as this emphasizes the illustrative powers of the novel which even the most eloquent histories cannot exercise. Take as example the matter of absentee landlordism. Here . . . it exists, balefully, no longer an idea but a whole, living institution, expanded to life size and set before us for observation." This illustrative power holds for the works of Dos Passos, Faulkner, Joyce, Caldwell, Wolfe, etc. We would be glad if a profounder view were brought to bear on the areas of tragedy of contemporary life presented in these books, as is done for instance in the works of foreign writers like Wassermann, Mauriac, Bernanos. We are aware that the craving for distinction and gain, the gratification of lust or cruelty, and a defeatist spirit of vindictiveness toward society count in varying degrees in the work of these writers. But we also see in their works documents written with extraordinary talent out of the infernos of our time, significant experiments in literary art, and some of our most trenchant criticism, both explicitly and by implication, of society today. Where is the same material being wrestled with by the "noble tradition"?

When we lament the fact that the new poet, the new dramatist and the new novelist, indeed the new generation, have taken their wrestling with ethical issues and value issues outside the church and outside the older framework of middle-class Puritan morality, we would very likely receive some such answer as the following. We may imagine an Eliot, an Aiken, an E. E. Cummings, an Evelyn Scott or a W. H. Auden speaking:

At a certain period in my twenties, I woke up one morning with a clear realization that my salvation depended upon escaping from my type, the type of Anglo-Saxon non-conformity in which I was brought up. I felt it suddenly—though after prolonged unrest and query—as a matter of spiritual life or death. This type appeared to me for what it was: a hemmed-in pietism, a combination of legalism and religious sentimentality, lacking in vast particulars. Item one, on the aesthetic side: lacking in the training of the senses and appreciation of the sensuous, with accompany tabus on art, whether historical or contemporary; insensitivity to beauty of worship, and acquiescence in crass manners (rather in the town, however, than in the country). Item two, on the side of the physical nature: lacking in a positive interpretation of the bodily life, physical beauty and its adornment, and a positive interpretation of the life of the sexes. Not only that but ridden by a negative view in this area that bears its fruit of distortion and suffocation of the sexual life in individuals, and social persecution. Item three, on the intellectual side: showing a disregard for the God-given faculty of intelligence, and for the primary functions of speculation and skepticism, either subordinating these to dogma or to pragmatic and utilitarian ends, or being sheerly incurious and unalert. Item four, on the side of general culture: obscurantist and narrow, ruling out whole worlds of Christian or pagan significance, whether Catholic or Oriental or classical. Item five, on the social-political side: unaware of, incurious as to the factors involved, living in a naïve and hooded ignorance of the tides of social forces upon which their temporary security rides; restricting all obligations to a personal code and resenting any obligations suggested by the total picture.

However unjust such a picture of Anglo-Saxon religious

culture might be, it is true enough in parts to illuminate the rebellion of many, and to indicate that such rebellion often is motivated by ethical protest and not by the desire for license.

One of the most striking features of the new poetry is the frequent note of nostalgia for more heroic ages in the past, contrasted with the shabby present. "The only functional difference," says MacLeish, "between Eliot's classical allusions and Milton's is that Milton's stones were chosen to embellish the edifice he was building while Eliot's were chosen to betray the tragic shoddiness of his time. The great stones at Palmyra shoulder through the Arab huts with just such brutal and contemptuous despair."[2] This theme of living today in a world from which stature and grace have departed is a theme found in some of the best work of Ezra Pound as well. Of course it is ever recurrent in history, but in the years after 1914 it takes a special form. It is not only the scorn felt by the artist for the Philistine, the diatribe against the "hucksters." Æ's *Iron Age*, for instance, belongs to the earlier mood in content and form:

> How came this pigmy rabble spun,
> After the gods and kings of old,
> Upon a tapestry begun
> With threads of silver and of gold?
> In heaven began the heroic tale
> What meaner destinies prevail! . . .
>
> O whether devil planned or no,
> Life here is ambushed, this our fate,
> That road to anarchy doth go,

[2] *Public Speech and Private Speech in Poetry*, p. 539.

This to the grim mechanic state.
The gates of hell are open wide,
But lead to other hells outside.

D. H. Lawrence also attacks the "grim mechanic state" from his own point of view. But the proper nostalgia of the modernist is something unique. It is marked by a sense that not only the public life but the inner life is given over to the banal, the empty, the barren. Much of Eliot's earlier work revolves about this theme. It is not merely a witty satire, nor the superciliousness of an intellectual, nor a sentimental nostalgia. It is a desperate irony testifying directly to a moral demand on life and bringing a civilization to judgment. For instance in "Gerontion" the old man sardonically notes the sordid setting of his last days, but over against it in his memory recur flashes of supernatural beauty and stature to reproach him or to elicit his protest to life. Yet the theme of remorse and humiliation are determining:

After such knowledge, what forgiveness? Think now
History has many cunning passages, contrived corridors
And issues, deceives with whispering ambitions,
Guides us by vanities . . .

Yet despite all these traps and seductions that life presents to us, we are not guiltless. For we have had knowledge of the imperishable splendor of how "came Christ the tiger," of the Last Supper, of "Hagakawa, bowing among the Titians," and personal memories that pierce the heart:

After such knowledge, what forgiveness?

Here we are on the threshold of the awed supplications of *Ash Wednesday*.

One can point out such evidences of an ethical judgment passed on the world and on themselves in many circles among the poets. As is to be expected it is conspicuous in the social revolutionary group. Auden characterizes the cheapness of the age in the warning to a bride who would settle in the old English hall, which, alas, is no longer the same:

> . . . One of the new
> Trunk-roads of fear passes the very door,
> And greed's thin cafés spring up overnight.
> The sham ornamentation of the feelings,
> The strident swimming-pool of the senses, thoughts
> Dressed up identically in townee smartness . . .[8]

The new power of the poets to bring their indictments and confessions home to the ordinary mortal is evident on every hand. They use the details of everyday life, colloquial language, metaphors taken from the routines and proper-ties of contemporary existence. Thus in Auden's poem above, the trunk-road, the café, the swimming-pool, all, it is to be observed, used symbolically, just as the "hall" itself is symbolical for the ancestral way of life. Eunice Clark in a poem "Take-off by the Medicine Closet" uses the detail of a crowded bathroom and the furtive scrutinies and dosings and garglings that go on there as a pointer to more serious lustrations:

> The purgatives along the shelf
> Miss the most poisonous deposits;

[8] "Poem," in *New Verse*, No. 9 (June 1934), p. 12.

Your face glows back but not your very self
From mirrored closets.

No lotion, potion, yeast or cream,
Will clear the clotted soul's complexion,
No tube of unguent here will soothe, no steam
Burst your infection . . .[4]

Such imagery is not pleasant or poetical, but it reminds Everyman of today of his ethical liabilities in a "public speech" that he can understand.

There is a tendency in the neocommunist poets to indict without confessing, that is, to blame. This is a more superficial note than the humiliation we were speaking of in connection with Eliot. For to censor others is essentially to dissociate ourselves from them and to relieve ourselves of responsibility for and with them. Much of the ingenuous revolutionary enthusiasm and indignation is of this irresponsible kind. It makes its task easier, as it thinks, by bedeviling the whole bourgeois world (this is easier than to seek out its allies there and to maintain the bonds of understanding), but by so doing it makes its task impossible. It has been well pointed out moreover that while these poets talk much of love and comradeship, the warm emotion of hate is a more available motive power often. Yet we must do the best of them justice, and also recognize that mixed motives are not confined to revolutionaries.

The deeper note of humility and remorse is the most significant feature of the ethical outlook of the poets. The age is passing from bitterness and malediction to self-knowledge.

[4] *The New Republic*, July 13, 1938, p. 273.

We are more acquainted with misgivings,
And more resigned to them, than you are yet.
Ours have all hatched, and are consuming us
Inside, young man. We set ourselves to grow
In the wrong earth, and soon we had no roots.

The later poems of E. A. Robinson from one of which, *Amaranth*, the above is quoted, are of inexhaustible interest at this point. Their significance has been commonly missed, but they illuminate with great power the modern situation of scrupulous and sensitive men canvassing their failure. They are most frequently colloquies of half-discerned souls in a twilight of damnation—clairvoyant, acid, sometimes bitter, sometimes chastened. These are like Dante's souls in the Inferno that suffer the slow rain of burning flakes of fire which symbolize tormenting memories and remorse. Such things *are* in the citadels of lives that have left ruin in their wake, and the discovery of it is data of immense consequence for moderns that had disbelieved in responsibility. The figure of Amaranth in the poem that has that title is a personage or spirit that haunts all men, meeting them fully at certain crises to give them disabused self-knowledge, a disclosure that overwhelms them or drives them to suicide. Meeting his eyes "that might have been the eyes of death, if death were life," men were either reborn or broken. In any case they are humble:

We are the reconciled initiates,
Who know that we are nothing in men's eyes
That we set out to be—and should have been,
Had we seen better. We see better now.

In this poem the particular sins repented of are those of
artist, preacher and lawyer, particularly the idolatries of
the artist. The idolatries of the flesh are repented of in
the deepest notes of much of the literature. The last
idolatory of the modern is that of science and the un-
rebuked *ubris* of man's approach to nature. Altogether it
is the mood of many today to admit the charge that is
brought in *Amaranth* against Atlas, the painter,

> I told him once
> What a crude opulence of mortality
> There was in what he did.

Our time is haunted not only by a sense of spiritual stature in the past, and misgivings for its own infatuations,
but also by the great ideal of love in its Christian sense.
The necessity of love has been brought home to it on the
one hand by the starving and frigid loneliness of much
of modern life, and on the other hand by conflict, chaos
and suffering that result from a cult of individualism or
mere tribalism. The inevitableness of love as a norm of
life, despite its difficulty, is being made clear *in experience*, empirically, and men do apprehend it when it comes
thus from life rather than from dogma or scripture.

Mr. MacLeish's poem, "Pole star for this year" in his
volume *Public Speech*, gives a graphic picture of the chaos
of values today when

> All truth alters and the lights
> Of earth are out . . .

He shows how the best values of the west have led to

violence and carnage, and that good men have been misled into inhumanity by their mocking faiths. One pole star remains in our bewilderment, that of love, but it is a particular kind of love,

> Love that hardens into hate—
> Love like hatred and as bright.

That is it has steel in it and is self-critical. It is the love of the surgeon or of the man that deals with the insane. In brief it is like the love of God who for his own reasons does not spare man. MacLeish's "Speech to those who say Comrade" follows with its similar warning that love is not the easy thing that comes by common blood but that it is won by common dangers endured.

W. H. Auden confirms this realization that love is great but not easy. Brother Every calls our attention in this connection to lines from *The Ascent of F6* by Auden and Isherwood:

> True, Love finally is great,
> Greater than all; but large the hate,
> Far larger than Man can ever estimate.
>
> But between the day and night
> The choice is free to all, and light
> Falls equally on black and white.

Perhaps our best evidence of this theme, however, may be taken from a novel published in 1931, Evelyn Scott's *A Calendar of Sin.*[5] One of the characters, Maurice, in a

---

[5] New York, Jonathan Cape and Harrison Smith, 1931, Vol. II, pp. 429 ff.

disillusioning hour in which the unreality and irresponsibility of a long liaison are suddenly brought home to him exclaims: "Why had he staked everything on what he knew to be illusion—knew it all the time? If the term 'love' had any real validity, the understanding of it must be slow, requiring every faculty to make it grasped. The way of love—if there was one—must be as difficult as that to any other truth. Why, then, he, like all the others, asking to be drunk with truth—as if the truth has ever come to men through drunkenness? And in the churches, as in the streets and brothels, everyone the same—all asking for the miracle that, without any assistance of discipline or honest ardour in themselves, would bring the truth! Love, if it can ever be achieved, he thought, would be as little the result of accident and vague excitement as the finest work of art. It would be something clear—a new light with which you could read the world—and the whole experience of sense and intellect would be a part of it."

CHAPTER XV

REVOLUTIONARY AND PROLETARIAN POETRY: KENNETH PATCHEN

We have had occasion a number of times to call attention to the fact that one school of the new writers should not be included in the cult of negation. This is the group whose concern is with social revolution. They share the social realism indeed; they are negative as regards any future for present society; they have also fallen heir to many of the disillusionments and bitter knowledge of the modern mood; they recognize the rootlessness of our culture; they have, finally, been influenced by the changes in poetic speech and method. But they have not been concerned with the personal problem or the psychological issues, nor with finding some individual Nirvana or return to nature. These are extroverts and their alternative to orthodoxy is devotion to a new social order.

This is a younger generation than the one to which Eliot, Pound, Aiken, Yeats belong. It came up after the war. In England its members were at the universities in the middle twenties. Their particular organ *New Verse* appeared around the beginning of the thirties, and the names that have drawn particular attention have been those of W. H. Auden, Stephen Spender, C. Day Lewis, MacNeice, Madge. They have wished to fight free from the defeatism and demoralization of the post-war years.

The predicament of Europe after the Peace Treaty, of Britain with its great strikes and unemployment, the paralysis of remedial efforts in the face of competitive capitalism and vested interests, as they saw it, and the challenge of the Russian experiment led them to their gospel of a new order. The development of fascism and of Hitler clarified and intensified their zeal. They became more than ever convinced of the view supported whether by Marx or Spengler or such Catholic writers as Dawson and Maritain or an Orthodox writer like Berdyaev, that Western society was breaking up, its organic bonds of common faith and morale lost, its inner conflicts constituting an incurable anarchy, and its men and women infected with sickness.

Much of this diagnosis they took over from the new poets before them but they made of it a social program and a poetic creed. They also took over the new "public speech" and colloquial style of address. But their lyrical optimism as to the new society inevitably reminds one of the social enthusiasm of Tennyson or Whitman, and their ardor for, and even participation in, the cause of the Spanish loyalists recalls Byron and Shelley. Today with the tragic ambiguity of the U.S.S.R. they have dissociated their revolutionary conceptions somewhat from the Russian formula, though they have not been really identified at any time with the actual proletarian communists in the latter's task of precipitating social strife. As intellectual revolutionaries, like Strachey or the Christian communists, their task has been one of education. Their poetry is made up in part of satirical criticism of the "old world" now as they conceive it, going to pieces, and of calls to sacrifice to the new world, and poetic forecasts of its values. Much of this takes the form of brilliant pamphleteering and topical verse rather than lyrical or personal poems. Here it falls in the tradition of the broadsheet. More recently Auden and Isherwood have written satirical plays or extravaganzas like *The Dog Beneath the Skin*. But they also produce more deeply matured and personal work. William Rose Benét, in reviewing Auden's recent book, *On This Island*, says, "Mr. Auden writes out of the terror and tumult, disillusionment and anger, of his own day. He is profoundly concerned about the state of the world . . . His book, I should say, is a good deal concerned with the love between individuals perplexed and harried by love of mankind and the hope for a better social order so that it is snatched, as it were, amid perils and imminent treacheries." Some attention has been given in earlier chapters to Auden's charges against the old regime, and the ethical motives in his work.

In the United States similar conditions and the influence of the group have resulted in similar work. The numerous new poetry magazines and annuals show a considerable place given to such themes, and readers of *Poetry, A Magazine of Verse*, as well as of many of the liberal reviews, not to mention *The New Masses*, are acquainted with it. We have spoken of MacLeish's radio plays dealing with the Wall Street panic and with the coming of the dictators, as well as of his view of modern poetry as capable of a social role. Attention has also been called to a few poems in *Public Speech* in which he points to love as the "Pole

star for this year" and defines the meaning of the word
Comrade as something not determined by the blood.

Men are brothers by life lived and are hurt for it.[1]

The work of Miss Rukeyser has also been cited. It is especially to be noted that this group in America includes a
definite group of writers who are or have been themselves
workers out of workers' families. These are properly distinguished as proletarian poets since they write consciously
of their class.

It is ambiguous or misleading to speak of these types of
poetry as communist poetry. The larger part of it represents merely such a plea for justice and community as
any believer in the future and in mankind feels. It is
inevitable that such a social passion should see the matter
in terms of an old and a new order. The point at which
to raise queries is not over the matter of a change of orders
or even over the theme of revolution, which in some
aspects is an intrinsically Christian idea, but over the
concepts of man involved. The larger part of this work
appears to be inspired by motives of humanity whose
derivation from Christian values is unmistakable if unrecognized. What else can one say of such a theme as that
of Kenneth Patchen, the American proletarian poet:

> O be willing to wait no longer.
> Build men, not creeds; seed not soil—
> O raise the standards out of reach.
> New men, new world, new life.[2]

[1] "Speech to those who say Comrade."
[2] *Before the Brave* (New York, 1936), p. 18.

In so far as these poets represent an actual iconoclasm it must be remembered that the outlook of men is affected by the conditions of their life, and that the technological changes of the last century have deeply altered these. New conditions of living shake men's habitual loyalties and assumptions. We speak of the changes that came in the nineteenth century with the industrial revolution. But these changes continue. For techniques continue to advance. "Advancing, they not only transform the economic system and the social relationships entangled in it, they subtly and profoundly change the scheme of values. Authority may resist the frontal attack of heresy or repair the schisms that it causes, but neither the secular nor the spiritual sword is potent against the habituations and attitudes that respond to new ways of earning a livelihood, to the manipulation of new mechanical powers, to the new resources, new luxury, new leisure, new freedom, and new servitude that their exploitation brings with it, and to the new relations between men and groups of men that they engender . . . new technology, by changing the basis of life, prepares for a change in the very basis of thought. It is thus of particular potency in undermining the established notions of authority held by the masses of men."[3]

The making of a communist is well seen in the case of a young intellectual, whom Charles Plisnier, the Belgian writer, describes in his book *Faux-Passeports*, a book which recently took one of the highest French prizes. The book is transparently autobiographical in many features. In an introduction written for that book but

[3] R. M. MacIver, "The Historical Pattern of Social Change," in *Authority and the Individual*, Cambridge, Mass., pp. 150, 151.

only published in its entirety in a review,[4] the author reviews the forces that played on him during his studies in
law at Brussels in 1919. To appreciate the revulsions he
felt toward various aspects of the status quo is to understand much of the new poetry.

When I try to picture what was going on in me I find various sharply contradictory sentiments: a violent antipathy
towards that contented mediocrity which exhibited itself on
every face; a hatred for the hate to which I had accustomed
myself during the war . . . an abhorrence for the disordered
scheme of life that met my eyes in the sordid prosperity of the
rich, the sordid resignation of the poor, and that acceptance
by both of values that could not possibly lead to the satisfaction of all; a thirst to see this abominable disorder changed;
a need to discover something to which one could give oneself
without reserve; an attitude of religious awe towards the Russian revolution . . . the intoxicating illusion that one found
in Marx a complete and coherent explanation of the whole
terrestrial globe, past, present and future. As a matter of fact,
I always said that I came to communism by way of the doctrine, but I know now that what decided me were the mournful aspects of life as it was: a working-girl dazzled by false
jewelry, the complacent look on the face of some half-washed
delivery boy, the line in front of a moving-picture theatre,
everything that showed the bourgeoisie luring the poor with
its crass materialism and appetite for perdition . . . I wanted
to break with that hateful hierarchy that made me one of the
privileged, with that culture whose overthrow I desired.

Such sentiments need not lead to a communist profes-
sion. In the case of the character who speaks in this book
it did so, but only for a period. He was unable to maintain

[4] Souvenirs d'un agitateur, *ESPRIT*, 6e année, 65 (1er février 1938),
pp. 723 ff.

complete obedience to the party. He still had scruples about his "duty of sincerity." He was not afraid for his skin but they wanted him to throw away with equal alacrity "what he called his honor." He felt perhaps that by comparison with the devoted extremists and martyrs, the "hard," he was only a sentimentalist, a poet who had made an imperfect renunciation. A stern friend had said to him, "You, comrade, take the Party for a house: go in one day, leave another day when you please. The Party is no more a house than the Church is. There are houses in the Party as there are houses in the Church. But like the Church the Party is a fellowship of flesh and spirit . . . The civil wars, the blood-conflicts have given it this religious character . . ."

The writer disavowed his communism half-heartedly but what especially interests us here is his account of how he was led to rebellion against the status quo. Through the war and through observation of the life about him and through study of economic laws he felt he had received a kind of clairvoyance with regard to society, insights into the shallowness not to say viciousness of social orthodoxy. Note what a considerable part in his decision against his class is made up of ethical motives. The scorn for materialism, the hot resentment against irresponsible privilege, the sick-heartedness over the corruption of the workers by commercialism and the loss of their simplicity by the peasants; these are ethical protests. The true Marxist goes on to cap it all with an economic doctrine and a program of action. Some of the new poets go on to this. But all or most share the clairvoyant revulsion from traditional life as they see it.

The work of Mr. Kenneth Patchen in his volume *Before the Brave*[5] is of great interest for the light it throws on the outlook of the "proletarian poet" or social radical today, and also for the parallels that appear in it with intense religious motivation. Large parts of it are of extreme difficulty. This is only partly due to the special character of his concerns and his imagery. One would hazard the guess that he has put himself to school to Hart Crane as any poet well may, and he shows some of the powers as well as some of the defects of that method. At his best, and his best is often struck out of a context of obscurity, we find a forcibleness of statement and an eloquence in its kind that indicate a gifted poet. And we may add to this the fact that Mr. Patchen in the frame of reference of his social themes touches deep levels of general human concern. We are not surprised to hear that in his subsequent work still in progress he has sought wider themes, without however abandoning his former sympathies.

The difficulties of the proletarian artist are illustrated well by this case. Mr. Patchen's volume which we shall analyze deals with the mission, the brotherhood, the sacrifices and elation of those who are the spearhead of the new order in the world today. Its intensity and its horizons grow out of the realities of the class struggle. Yet the poet cannot safely read his cause and his allies in terms of the actual class struggle or the actual working classes or the actual political and social front. He will find himself disappointed and betrayed by the workers or by the U.S.S.R. or by the Internationals and his cause will not be theirs.

[5] New York, 1936. Mr. Patchen has more recently had published *First Will and Testament*, Norfolk, Conn., 1939.

The revolutionary poet must therefore be on his guard not only against the old order, but also against his comrades. Mr. Patchen gives evidence of this in some private notes he has furnished on his present position in which he shows that the writer should keep himself clear of passing phases whether in the social conflict or the literary scene.

"It is not easy for me to formulate a credo in regard to 'the poet and the class struggle.' No contemporary poet (or critic) has evidenced a consistent attitude towards any major human problem; he has occupied himself with literary-and-political jockeying for position—not content with changing horses in the middle of the stream, he must change the stream as well; he has spent his energies baying at the moon and mooning at the bay. There is little to go on.

"No poet can write 'for the people' without realizing that current literary tastes (in the hands of the money-changers) have little to do with literature; i.e., Burns, Heine, Homer, etc.

"Jesus Christ is still a better subject for the poet than the emasculated Lenin of the Stalinists . . .

"Let the poet be one with his own life.

"Let him read more Dante and Burns and less political mouth-frothing . . .

"Influences of my life in a steel-worker's home on my work and outlook:

"In the beginning, at least, it gave me a contempt for intellectual writers who intellectualized but did not write —still have it.

"Made me suspicious of people who 'loved the working class.' The working class, by reason of its position in this

society, is base, treacherous, ignorant and *cheap*; to say
otherwise is to enter upon a major contradiction. The middle class is worse, of course, and still more so, the
upper . . ."

Patchen states that he is at work on a new poem of exceptional length and adds: "I am afraid that it doesn't
have a great deal to do with 'proletarian' writing. I am
rather bitter about the present set-up in that direction."

We can well understand the objection that a writer like
Patchen must feel to have his name bandied about as a
"proletarian" poet. He is not interested in being classified,
and his convictions are too serious for him to enjoy being
made the object of literary gossip. He must go his own
way disabused as to both right and left but not discour-
aged. One of the unexpected notes that recurs in the midst
of his bitterest denunciations is a wistful appeal for love
or a call to forgiveness. With such an ideal haunting him
we can well believe that he finds himself at times disappointed.

There can be no mistaking, however, the ardor and
austerity of his challenge to whoever will hear, be they
proletarians or not. Nor can one mistake the true doctrine
of communism, which appears in his work not as doctrine
but as singing and passion. For those who know the language and those that will penetrate the difficulties, here
are the themes that have moved mountains in Russia and
that work as a well-nigh irresistible ferment in many parts
of the world today. This is the faith and the uncom-
promising boldness of a *church*, but of a church that is a
church indeed. Let the guardians of religious institutions
and of democracy with their relaxed powers and slackened

bows give good heed. Do they believe in the future? Here in any case is certainty of inevitable and predestined victory. Do they recognize the mortal conflict of good and evil? Here is deliberate preparation for the imminent revolution. Do they have the elate abandonment of apostle and martyr? Do they touch hands in a sense of common mission with committed bands in many nations? Here is this kind of vocation and this kind of solidarity together with a sense of glory growing out of ignominy and triumph won out of despair.

Far carrying movements in the world rise ultimately out of conditions where the hearts of men are plowed and harrowed for long periods of time by humiliation and distress. The iron enters into the soul finally and they become capable of single-mindedness. They become capable of disregarding inconsequentials like comfort and safety. This condition among the poor is evidenced in these poems of Patchen:

> their retching sour rage
> Is splendid harvest. (p. 110)

The ignominies, deprivation and injury reach a point where profound hungers and urges are felt, not necessarily destructive, but in any case insistent. Not necessarily destructive: it is first of all a crying out for something better, and only if that is denied comes the necessity to destroy the barriers to something better:

> Let us have madness openly, O men
> Of my generation. Let us follow
> The footsteps of this slaughtered age . . .

But note what follows:

> We wanted more; we looked to find
> An open door, an utter deed of love,
> Transforming day's evil darkness . . . (p. 41)

And again,

> We should love but cannot love being as we are. (p. 97)

As the proletarian thinks of a comrade murdered and another lynched and others in other lands shot down by the Fascists he is driven to prefer open revolution to the hopeless inaction of the present interim:

> better to die better to feel that all wisdom
> science and mastery have been turned against
> you that they notice you and kill you . . .
> better to die while heavy guns shake the
> earth and it's all big and clear   save us
>   from the peace between
> wars   Fool fool every man's at war who's
>   hungry and hunted whether
> in Omaha or Tokyo here they come. Here
>   they come. Look out
> they mean business they mean an end to standing
>   in rain waiting for freights out of
>   Toledo and Detroit. Did we ever make
> a town? a porterhouse?   we were always just
>   this side of getting anything
> or anywhere . . .
>   a hundred million of us coming
> up those stairs in Spain in Mexico in India . . .
>   millions ready
> to break the back of this muddle-born world. (pp. 103 ff.)

For the revolutionary the outcome is certain. Here we have the Marxian version of early Christian apocalyptic with its imminent and predestined triumph. This is what "all Time has willed."

>   Do watch! do wait! the season nears its grain.   (p. 77)

Yet sometimes the interim appears long. It is like a sultry day when the awaited thunder storm holds off:

>   Now this remains: the thunder stopped;
>   the stubborn sky grown thick,
>   all clumsy, holding back . . .
>   this nasty
>   waiting being everything in one, a civil
>   war in perfect check
>   and then
>   the rain! (p. 85)

At times the days of "the major operation" appear at hand:

>   Chiefly I prize this loss of patience, deep
>   In riot days around us; these swollen
>   Times propel the future forward: tear
>   Alike my friends and turn about my foes.
>   I think not every lesson learned
>   is
>   Full of welcome: weeds in suburban streets;
>   Stalking gangs who fire at sight . . .
>   These withered times prepared no turkish-bath
>   Of comradeship or endless singing in the square . . . (p. 14)

If we ask what the ultimate goal is we find the question waived in a poem called "Graduation." The end of work in other people's industry and world, dancing in the palaces of king and "patriot," the release of prisoners, victories and economic gain: can there be more than this? Perhaps, but it is enough that "the program's under way." Away with speculation.

We've learned that consummation waits
And will not rot. O let your Love consume your thought.
(p. 83)

But what is under way

    starts wheels going worlds growing
and any man can live on earth when we're through
    with it. (p. 35)

To be of the pioneers in this revolutionary procedure is to meet the truncheons of the police, Midwestern jails, tear gas and riot guns. The usual foreshortening of the interim between us and the millennium means that the crisis is imminent and that one lives in the anticipation of martyrdom. Yet without sentimentality.

    We will no martyrs or legends.
    We can't get there by taxi-cab or sentiment. (p. 17)

Nevertheless, there is a sense of vocation which gives significance to the role of those who go forward to barrage and barricade: they are "conquerors of time and men,"

    Models for a better maker, propellers of a surer motion,
    Masters in a stricter sense—alive or dead . . .

We are that thing for which we fight.
We are the deepest task of centuries; lucky
To stand where we stand, hardy
To weather all they can give who have taken
The every weight of a more hopeless war
    since the day we were born. O we are not
Afraid of wounds we've always had. O death
Is a minor thing to those who've never lived. (p. 107)

This hardihood is related to the conditions of life of the workers. As a result of the long underworld existence they have not only the bodies but the tempering and the abandonment to be invincible.

we're not pretty we're as ugly as hell coming out of the holes
they dug for us to live in we're proud of our hardness
we've been picked to live because we could not die
they could not kill us even when our own were turned
against us they cannot make a dent in the iron faces
we've grown in the cellar of the world we've got
no pretty job to do we are the ugly logic whose beautiful
bones shall be the frame of all the body of wonder
which we can never know. (p. 125)

The single-mindedness is reinforced by a mystical sense of community with comrades throughout the world who suffer or die, whether famous martyrs like Lauro de Bosis or the unknown. The resolute mood is maintained not by "words or dying themes Of flag or wooden guns": they are

a legion whose skill
Is best put forth by order of a public bond
In blood we've lost on every field of earth and sea.

And this vocation and solidarity in deprivation and crisis is one of elation, as the same poem says,

> our country is the careless star in man. (p. 78)

This theme is best brought out in the account of an execution, "Joe Hill Listens to the Praying." While the chaplain prays, and while the rifles are prepared, the mind of the condemned goes back to the dramatic hours of the social struggle in which he has taken part, various indomitable if forlorn apostles of the cause, the casual laborer's life, the "bumming" over the great West in midsummer, the bounty and freshness of earth to these free spirits that had taken their lives in their hands, the epic incidents of strike and courtroom, whose epic character had all the more moving quality for the unequal odds and the Main Street setting.

> The homeless, the drifters, but, our songs
>   had hair and blood on them.
> There are no soap boxes in the sky.
> We won't eat pie, now, or ever
>   when we die,
>   but Joe
> We had something they didn't have:
>   our love for these States
>   was real and deep . . .
> Let them burn us, hang us, shoot us,
>   Joe Hill,
> For at the last we had what it takes
>   to make songs with. (p. 120)

It is a most important and a very delicate task to analyze

the social judgments that underlie such rebellion. One cannot but respond to the passionate aspirations that voice themselves in it. The devotion to what until now at least has been a forlorn hope in this country is a rebuke to the orthodox in church and state, so inclined to rest on their oars even in times of evident social distress. Even among those that are not communists there is a widespread revulsion against the values of pre-war middle-class life, patriotism as then viewed, and the church. We have seen in most of our modernist poetry that many have been shaken in their confidence in these attitudes and institutions. The aspects of our American order that a worker like Patchen meets are often such as to make understandable the absoluteness of his verdict. We cannot but recognize moreover that where citadels of entrenched and arbitrary power establish themselves—and they establish themselves in all orders—the play of social forces cannot but lead to such crises and overturns as he envisages.

Precise estimates, however, of the good and bad of social institutions and forces is not easy. Whether they are such as to forbid hope of prompt peaceful correction needs more insight and competence than most men have. In particular our supposed disinterested indignation is often complicated by hidden motives of a personal kind. As Robert Frost has suggested there is a vast difference between grief and grievances. Capitalistic culture is, indeed, cursed with a curious stuntedness and complacency which will drive the critic to every form and degree of disgust and lead him to spew out every feature of its arts. But an objective judgment upon anything as complex as a human society is possible to few. The wisdom of such

social judgments and such class aversion is only propor-
tional to the amount of love for mankind that the critic
brings to them. Otherwise he is making an obscure series
of transferences of personal grievances to an imagined
social order, and is moving in allusions and fictions. And
such is the basis of most Marxism and class conflict. And
such is the basis of a certain amount of the art and poetry
of proletarian or collectivist inspiration, and of the modernist revolt generally. In so far, it is given its life by
illusions and is soon exposed. But if a critic loves and
understands men he will not confuse the abiding ills of
life nor his personal grievances with the ills of a particular social order. He will then be able to pass an illuminating judgment on his day. Of course elements of such
sound reaction are found in our poets, and the modernist
literature partakes of good and bad. We do not mean that
an ideal critic or artist should take a remote and inactive
view of the social order, but that there are few Isaiahs or
Lincolns who may permit themselves a dogmatic view or
the right to hate or the licence of withering denunciation.
The pure fire of zeal is too mixed with the fumes of bitterness in all of us. It is notable that in the personal communication from Patchen quoted above, he shows himself
disabused of any over simple assignment of right and
wrong in the issue between the classes, and that a plea
for solutions in terms of love rather than violence recurs.

CHAPTER XVI

W. B. YEATS AND THE CHRISTIAN OPTION

For the poets the scandal of Christ is his asceticism. The very medium of their art as poets; indeed, the very element of their experience as men, is the gamut of human living, emotions, drama. "Man's resinous heart" and the loves, loyalties, the pride, the grief it feeds—these are the stuff of poetry and the sense of life. And the Cross lays its shadow on this; it draws away all the blood from the glowing body of existence and leaves it mutilated and charred in the hope of some thin ethereal felicity. The wine of life is changed to water. The spectrum, incredibly enough, is surrendered for an undifferentiated and commonplace white light. The "dramatic caves" of the human heart and imagination are renounced for some wan empyrean of spiritual revery. The very word "spiritual" has come to signify inanity and vacuity. The refusal of religion by the modern poet, and by more than moderns and by more than poets, goes back to the apparent denial of human living by religion, to the supposed incompatibility of life with Life and of art with faith.

One can see the dialogue that man holds with himself over the issue going on in the nobler poets and writers. The theme is recurrent in the French novel. "Christ would have all of man; the fundamental evil, therefore, is concupiscence. Yet human nature is so constituted that, ex-

cepting for the greatest saints, there is no escape from
desire . . . the resolve to follow the Saviour is the fundamental, inescapable business of man; but . . . man cannot pursue this business without ceasing to be human.
The sharpness with which the dilemma is stated may be
unreasonable, but it is contemporary."[1] Becket in *Murder
in the Cathedral* knows that to the human point of view
his martyrdom will seem

> Senseless self-slaughter of a lunatic,
> Arrogant passion of a fanatic . . .

But a peculiarly interesting case of this dialogue is
W. B. Yeats, early a pagan, always a pagan, of the noblest
kind, but one touched repeatedly by scruple he is not inclined to conceal. He takes his leave of the great Catholic,
Von Hügel, with an explanation that his role of poet
predestines him to his unbelief—only out of the lion can
come forth sweetness:

> . . . I—though heart might
> find relief
> Did I become a Christian man and choose for
> my belief
> What seems most welcome in the tomb—play
> a predestined part.
> Homer is my example and his unchristened heart.
> The lion and the honeycomb, what has Scripture said?
> So get you gone, Von Hügel, though with blessings on your
> head.[2]

The implication is that a Christian so sterilizes his

---

[1] George N. Shuster, "François Mauriac," in Zabel, *op. cit.*, p. 450.
[2] "Vacillation, VIII," *Collected Poems* (New York, 1937), p. 290.

heart that there is no concern left for art and the rich play, the riot and fecundity of life. The lion is changed to a lamb. It is as though the only treasury of poetry was "the lust of the flesh, and the lust of the eyes, and the pride of life." As Yeats writes,

> From man's blood-sodden heart are sprung
> Those branches of the night and day
> Where the gaudy moon is hung.[3]

Why, it will be asked, does not Yeats recognize that poetry and the arts have flourished in the church of Von Hügel? That Christianity has known how to penetrate life and make a world in which human instincts and energies have not been sterilized but rather enriched?

But the poet knows his enemy better perhaps than it knows itself. He knows that a conversion would be no mere easy sublimation of his pagan beauty and truth. He knows that rightly understood it would involve a certain cruel asceticism. Roots would have to be torn out for new roots to grow. It would involve an asceticism like that of Hopkins renouncing his gift—paralleled even by the pagan Rimbaud. Or one like that of Fargo in E. A. Robinson's *Amaranth* who destroys his own paintings, "an oily-fiery sacrifice of one day," and so has become free:

> Art has no rest
> Until, unlike the old guard, it surrenders,
> Or, like the old guard, dies. He had surrendered,
> So not to greet himself among the slain
> Before he should be dead.

[3] *Ibid.*, VI, p. 289.

Such a surrender need not mean the total relinquishment of an art, but from the unshriven point of view it might well appear the blasting of the whole territory out of which art comes. For Yeats the surrender to the faith of Von Hügel would mean, in any case, that he could thenceforth cast only a casual eye upon that whole tangle of human nostalgias, memories and passions which was the man Yeats and the poet Yeats, a legacy of a lifetime of pursuits, an identity shaped by decades of noble but pagan complacencies, a tangle of sentiment and outlook of which he was a prisoner.

We had fed the heart on fantasies.

He was at that late age indurated to a certain complex of thoughts and imaginations, honorable, yes, noble—yet of the earth, earthy, of the natural man. Thus he could continue only as the poet of "original sin" as he answers in reply to his scruple:

> The Soul. Seek out reality, leave things that seem.
> The Heart. What, be a singer born and lack a theme?
> The Soul. Isaiah's coal, what more can man desire?
> The Heart. Struck dumb in the simplicity of fire!
> The Soul. Look on that fire, salvation walks within.
> The Heart. What theme had Homer but original sin?[4]

These things we have in a figure applied to Yeats, not as though counting him exceptional, but as typical, indeed as the least vulnerable of many. The words addressed to the painter Atlas in *Amaranth* could be spoken to hosts of

[4] *Ibid.*, "Vacillation, VII," p. 290.

admirable contemporary secularists, and not only poets
and artists:

> I told him once
> What a crude opulence of mortality
> There was in what he did.[5]

Yeats is right, then, in recognizing the asceticism involved in a conversion. From the point of view of the
"unchristened heart" the renunciations called for appear
to have no compensations. The choice between pagan
and believer looks like the absolute antimony we have
mentioned between wine and water. The world and the
flesh must, indeed, be crucified in the Christian life, but
the pagan can hardly be expected to see that they come to
life in a new form, and that the christened heart has its
embodied creation, and its own manifold articulation as
well as the unchristened, and Isaiah and Dante have their
theme as well as Homer.

The alternative is again meditated by Yeats in his poem,
"The Choice":

> The intellect of man is forced to choose
> Perfection of the life, or of the work,
> And if it takes the second must refuse
> A heavenly mansion, raging in the dark . . .

That is, the artist chooses the work, and that means "the
day's vanity, the night's remorse," and, afterwards, the
"raging in the dark." But between the "pole" of the Cross
and the pole that symbolizes for Yeats the tent of the
Zodiac and the "glory of the earth and air" the attractions

[5] *Amaranth*, p. 30.

do not appear to be equal. But we should not think his unwillingness any sign of shallow incomprehension. He knows that

>   out of rock,
> Out of a desolate source,
> Love leaps upon its course . . .

and that

> 'Love has pitched his mansion in
> The place of excrement;
> For nothing can be sole or whole
> That has not been rent.'

The outcome of Yeats is, in ethics a noble traditional humanity, and in religious philosophy, a Platonism articulated earlier in terms of his Celtic symbolism. He has borne witness to the renewal of his creative powers in his old age by the help of this symbolism. The vision that came to him was one testified by the poems of *The Winding Stair* series (1933). The stain, "the fury and the mire," the frenzy, the world-besotted soul, birth upon birth, and death upon death—all these are resolved, taken up into silence, frozen into a trance. Blood begotten spirits here leave "all complexities of mire and blood." This is a world which has ever been.

> Things out of perfection sail,
> And all their swelling canvas wear,
> Nor shall the self-begotten fail
> Though fantastic men suppose
> Building-yard and stormy shore,
> Winding-sheet and swaddling-clothes.[6]

[6] *Ibid.*, "Old Tom Again," p. 309.

That such Platonism passes easily into a morally ambiguous monism is evident from several of the poems. This is after all the recurrent "way of life" of the artist: to transcend phenomena in an imaginative experience, and so to cherish such experiences as practically to encourage irresponsibility. Tate laments that "the fusion of human success and human error in a vision of the whole of life, *the vision itself being its own goal* (his italics), has almost disappeared from the world of the spirit." Looked at on one side, such an ideal is admirable. But it needs to be further defined lest it pass over into a doctrine of moral equivalence. The young Lauro de Bosis wrote a poem in which, in the vision of the whole, he saw his own grief compensated by the joy of others: while he was in the night the sun shone upon some more fortunate brother. This philosophy would lead one in privilege to endure with complacency the wretchedness of others. Fortunately, as in the case of de Bosis himself, one's instincts are often more humane than one's outlook. But the complacent vision of the whole of a young de Bosis can easily pass into the unreality of a young Mussolini who became lyric over the bombing of Ethiopian villages: sunlight and shadow are part of the total vision!

The ambiguity of the artist's quest has its supreme contemporary expression in Yeats' "Byzantium," to be read in connection with the accompanying poem, "Mohini Chatterjee." Here the poet reaches a vision of the whole of life in a detachment or a Nirvana which

> disdains
All that man is,

> All mere complexities,
> The fury and the mire of human veins.[7]

Such a passage, again, hangs on a knife-edge between a legitimate revulsion from the ravage and fury of life,

> That dolphin-torn, that gong-tormented sea,

and a doctrine of moral equivalence. The artist in this outlook leans toward that type of mystic whose religion is one of sub-personal ecstatic absorption. It is sub-personal and not supra-personal (Dante's *Paradiso*) because the bliss attained escapes rather than resolves the tragedies of the will, the tragedies of personal conflict. It is not enough therefore to say with Mr. Tate that the vision of the whole of life should be its own goal. It depends upon what vision. The vision of de Bosis is a false vision and this has something to do with the thinness of the imagination that works on it. The vision of "Byzantium" is a deeper one and one that nourishes the imagination more richly whether here or in the Upanishads. The vision of *The Divine Comedy* is still truer and offers still more to the poet. Thus "the true content of the world's phenomena" in such moments of total vision will differ as widely as poets and mystics have differed, and what one poet sees and communicates will be more or less "total," more or less true, and more or less significant for "the complexities of mire and blood" that the world's course represents.

Yeats is of that perennial race of the pagans who look to nature and the imagination for their faith and find there a resolution of life's multiplicity and contradictions in unity.

[7] *Collected Poems,* p. 285.

The sense of the *person* has not developed to the point where it opposes such monism, and the issues and values of the personal life have not advanced to the point where they, rather than nature and the imagination, become the clues to reality. Herein such a poet is typical of many of the noblest of our contemporaries. All the higher readings of life outside the Hebrew and Christian tradition tend to an elevated mystical pantheism of one form or another. Whether Hindu, Greek or Celt, transcendentalist or naïve theosophist, they have never grasped the primordial significance of the personal will, its insistent claim and its fatality. Therefore what would be for them a cosmos of responsible persons is seen as an impersonal masquerade of the One or of the *animus mundi*. In the case of Yeats we have a further commentary on that "numbness" to the intricacies of personal feeling which Mr. Winters has indicated as one of the limitations of all mystical poetry.

CHAPTER XVII

MR. T. S. ELIOT AND THE ANGLO-CATHOLIC OPTION

"*The Waste Land* was and is a summons to those who want a new or syncretic religion to explore the Christian Church. And since T. S. Eliot passed over the waste into the Church of England, it has become less and less possible for a modern English or American poet or novelist to neglect Christianity as altogether impossible of belief."[1] As this statement indicates, it would be a mistake to separate too sharply the Eliot of *The Waste Land* and the Eliot of *Murder in the Cathedral*. Both are saturated with Christian motives. A converted Christian, certainly one on the brink of Christianity, could write the former.[2] Only those for whom the waste land of the world is without tears and imprecations are truly unbelievers. It is a believer who finding himself in the Inferno knows it for exile. We can easily imagine a converted Christian writing *The Waste Land* in much the same way as Paul wrote the seventh chapter of Romans. The argument will always be renewed as to whether Paul was here recalling the desperation of the days before Damascus or whether he was describing the continuing desperation of the mortal state, though redeemed. Karl Barth says the latter. In any

[1] Brother George Every, *op. cit.*, p. 143.
[2] By the same token and by contrast they probably err who suppose that the O'Neill of *Days Without End* is a convert.

case the struggle of Flesh and Spirit and the paroxysms of his servitude were contemporary to Paul the Christian.

Nevertheless, the work of Eliot indicates an ascent of the stair—"*verso gli alti saliri*"—by degrees, at whatever point an overt affiliation was decided, and we have of late a writer whose themes fall on the positive side of his experience. He writes out of a double experience that peculiarly fits him to be an interpreter of life for our time, that double experience that Dante refers to in speaking of Trajan in Paradise:

> *ora conosce quanto caro costa*
> *non seguir Cristo, per l'esperienza*
> *di questa dolce vita e dell' opposta* (xx, 46-48)[3]

The sense of our condition is too chastened to find expression in an easy note of paean and lyricism. For all of us who have had a like history the present stage is one rather of the Purgatorio than the Paradiso. We do not lay claim to place in the seraphic chorus. Of the best we can do with our recovered energies we say,

> These fragments I have shored against
> my ruins.

Our ruins are all about us. The recurrent theme in Eliot's writings,[4] the one with which *The Waste Land* closes, fits us all:

> *Poi s'ascose nel foco che gli affina.*[5]

[3] now knoweth he how dear it costs, Christ not to follow, by his experience of this sweet life and of the opposite.
[4] Again recently in *The Family Reunion* (1939).
[5] There he hid him in the fire which refines them. *Purgatorio*, xxvi, 148.

That is, we impatiently recommit ourselves after every interruption to the searing flames of purification and judgment like Arnaut, "prompt to drink the sweet worm-wood of the torments,"

a ber la dolce assenzio de' martiri (*Purgatorio*, xxiii, 86)

The deepest literature of today is full of repentance as we have seen in connection with Robinson and Yeats. But while Gerontion can say,

> After such knowledge, what forgiveness?

the speaker of *The Waste Land* senses the infinite surpluses beyond his need, the "damp gust bringing rain" to his thirst. The boundary land is further the theme in "The Hollow Men." In "Journey of the Magi" the negative side of the solution is what is felt. To reach the manger is to find not so much a birth as a death.

> this Birth was
> Hard and bitter agony for us, like Death, our death.

This corroborates what we have said above in connection with Yeats as to the inevitable drastic asceticism of a conversion.

These poems with *Ash Wednesday* and the temptations in *Murder in the Cathedral* vividly present the painful struggle of grace and its foes. It is difficult to talk lightly of sin in terms of maladjustment in the presence of these poems. We have here the human heart attached to "lying images of good,"

imagini di ben seguendo false (*Purgatorio*, xxx, 131)

The prevailing figures and tone are those of Dante. There are five direct allusions to the *Divine Comedy* in *The Waste Land* alone. Those acquainted with Eliot's critical essays will recognize the evidently unique appeal for him of this poet. Prolonged consideration of the Cantos has done much to set the terms in which the religious problem has appeared to him. When we recall the influence of Dante in so different a way upon Mr. Ezra Pound we may well conclude that Dante is that major poet of the past who is most contemporary to our time, who best speaks to our condition, and who is most likely to have a great role in the spiritual growth of the future. We may note a number of aspects of Dante which make him eloquent to our ears.

Dante sees mortal men as ghosts or as spirits, already treading the burning marl or environed in the fire or the ice. This power to read men in terms of conscience and eternity rather than of flesh and blood we have seen in Francis Thompson, Geoffrey Scott and E. A. Robinson. For the last named it is highly characteristic in his later work. As for the more extremely disassociated poets of today, the very unreality of the world furthers this congeniality of Dante to them, even though they equally discount the reality of the self. They can make their own the words of Virgil to Statius in Purgatory:

> *Frate,*
> *non far, chè tu se' ombra, ed ombra vedi.*[6] (*Purgatorio*, xxi, 131, 132)

So Edmund Burke exclaimed, "What shadows we are and

[6] "Brother, do not so, for thou art a shade and a shade thou seest."

what shadows we pursue!" So Eliot, citing Dante, sees the
city throngs as phantoms:

> I had not thought death had undone so many.

Again, Dante views sin most often in terms of habitual
delusion, obsession, diseased fancy, madness or fever. He
is not moralistic or legalistic. Sin is sickness, even though
the personal contumacy be involved. There is a modern-
ness about this. Original sin is expressed in a way that
modern realism and modern psychology can understand.
In "Gerontion" there is one of the most striking passages
in all the work of Eliot. Alluding to the tree of the knowledge of good and evil and Adam's fall the poet notes their
consequence: such is the tragic anomaly and ambiguity of
our condition that, in effect, conscience itself is like a
spinning compass, of no avail. For we learn in life's experience to our consternation that our sins often lead us to
good and our virtues to unnatural crimes!

> These tears are shaken from the wrath-bearing tree.[7]

Thus, in any case, moderns see moral evil as in some
strange way inveterate and working destruction even
through good intentions.

For Dante evil acts through alienated minds, through
perverted imagination:

> *O insensata cura dei mortali* (*Paradiso*, xi, 1.)[8]
> *Ahi, anime ingannate* (*Paradiso*, ix, 10.)[9]

[7] *Poems, 1909-1925*, p. 52.
[8] "Insensate care of mortals."
[9] "Ah, souls deceived."

Sin is delirium. It is infatuation, whether that of pride,

> *O vanagloria dell' umane posse* (*Purgatorio*, xi, 91.)[10]

or that of gold, the

> *sacra fame*
> *dell'oro, l'appetito de' mortali*[11]

or the thirst for blood,

Sangue sitisti, ed io di sangue t'empio.[12] (*Purgatorio*, xii, 57.)

Sin also, therefore, is blindness:

> *Frate,*
> *lo mondo è cieco, e tu vien ben da lui*[13] (*Purgatorio*, xvi, 65,
> 66.)

And Christians like others are "sick in mental vision,

O superbi Christian miseri lassi,
che, della vista della mente infermi. (*Purgatorio*, x, 121, 122.)

Dante is seen congenial to our poetry again in his emphasis on experience, on personal history, on explorations
of the worlds, the lower and the higher ones. Virgil leads
him from circle to circle that he may have full experience
(*esperienza piena*). The type of this motive of spiritual
exploration in modern poetry is the *Anabase* of St. Leger,[14]

---

[10] "O empty glory of human powers!"
[11] "the cursed greed of gold, man's natural hunger."
[12] "For blood thou did'st thirst and with blood I fill thee."
[13] "Brother, the world is blind, and verily thou comest from it."
[14] St. J. Perse (St. Leger), *Anabase* (with a translation in English by
T. S. Eliot), (London, 1930).

but it recurs in much English and American work. And here too it is ultimately the same "peace" they seek which, Dante says,

di mondo in mondo cercar mi si face.[15] (*Purgatorio,* v, 63.)

Those worlds may be the submerged worlds of ancient culture that *The Waste Land* uncovers, or strange innei worlds of the psyche, but the theme of experience runs through all, and the sense of life's dimensions.

Thus the deeper terms of Eliot's view of purgation and freedom are found in Dante. In the literary expression of it we find other elements, especially a curious use of abstractions of a philosophical character. In "The Hollow Men" we may point to Section V, where the boundary condition is that

> Between the potency
> And the existence.

And in the Becket play there is the well-known cryptic statement by Thomas concerning "the wheel" and "the pattern" on which both the actor and the sufferer

> are fixed
> In an eternal action, an eternal patience.
> To which all must consent that it may be willed
> And which all must suffer that they may will it.

The former antithesis of potency and existence is characteristic of Dante, as of Aquinas and Aristotle, and is combined in Eliot's poem, as in Dante, with the Platonic

[15] "Makes me pursue it from world to world."

antithesis of idea and reality. But the latter antithesis of sufferer and actor is strange to the Divine Comedy. Dante is, indeed, often concerned with the problem of *moral* freedom and predestination, but the emphasis in this passage falls rather on the more general question of the freedom of the human agent in a world whose pattern is under the divine control. The superficial reader is likely to link Eliot's paradoxes here with the Indian theme of Emerson's "Brahma." These profound questions ever push the thinker upon paradox and ultimately to the point of speechlessness. But Emerson's poem teaches that there is, except superficially, no individual actor and no pattern; there is only the one Actor or Self, namely Brahma.

In the passage in Eliot, on the other hand, there is a real pattern which must subsist, and real actors who act and "suffer" (i.e., are "patient" in the etymological sense of being acted upon) by virtue of their personal identity. The passage is a notable attempt to relate dialectically and artistically the ideas of free will and God's sovereignty. The women of Canterbury voice their forebodings as they sense how they are being helplessly "drawn into the pattern of fate" and into participation in a great act of God. And Becket hearing it comments upon that pattern of fate *sub specie aeternitatis*: the eternal action of God is willed by God, but it is also willed by men. But here is the paradox: men's free consent follows from the fact that they "suffer," i.e., that they are subject to the action of God,

which all must suffer that they may will it.

The passage is more significant when applied to the act

of martyrdom of the saint rather than when applied to the condition of "the little people" in "their humble and tarnished frame of existence." For in his case further comment is found elsewhere in the play. The fate of Becket, the event or moment of his death, is looked on from both sides of the shield as a moment "out of time." It is a moment of the supernatural, both of God and the devil, out of time and out of space. Becket in his sermon says that "a martyrdom is never the design of man": it is the finger of God; the human instrument loses himself in the will of God. Or again,

> It is not in time that my death shall be known;
> It is out of time that my decision is taken
> If you call that decision
> To which my whole being gives entire consent.

But on the other hand, after the crime the chorus speaks:

> this is out of life, this is out of time,
> An instant eternity of evil and wrong.

This sounds more like the dialectical theology of today than the thought of Dante and Aquinas. We have the impression that Mr. Eliot has been reading Kierkegaard and Barth and that they here and there peer through the curtain. The terms are abstract rather than plastic and suggest a background of professional theological preoccupation.

In any case, whether the supernaturalism be Thomist or Barthian, the question is raised whether tragedy benefits or loses by it. One of the shrewdest comments we have heard on the play is that Becket's act of martyrdom being an effect of grace in which we are taken up out of the arena of human relations and conflicts, the essence of tragedy is absent. Aristotle's canon that the hero must not be too perfect is disobeyed. But more than that the hero is more, or less, than a man; he is in the final moment a puppet of grace. Against the background of Catholic supernaturalism and the Catholic doctrine of saints and martyrs, Becket's action is a miracle and not an act of heroism. The triumph is one of God, it is not an issue of human conflict. We have to do not with a "tragedy" but with a Miracle play. This view seems to us to be true. That particular pathos and drama that hang about the fate of a *man*, whether a good man that falls into tragic conflict with fate, or a man of mixed good and evil whose sins lead him to his downfall, that pathos, that sense of tears in human things, are not found here. By the same token the Passion of Christ can never be read as "tragedy." But if we cannot find this kind of appeal in *Murder in the Cathedral*, it has its own in large measure. Indeed, the first part of the action up through the temptation utilizes the values of tragedy, strictly so called. But more than that, what we have here, as in the gospels, is dramatic conflict, indeed, but it is the conflict of God and man, with the emphasis falling on God's action and its universal significance, and not upon the lot of the mortal protagonists. Jacob's wrestling with God is a different kind of drama and a different kind of overthrow and blessing from Hector's struggles with Achilles. The gods are participants in Greek tragedy but they are themselves finite, under Fate or Zeus, or if the ultimate Zeus appears it is so that the particular human drama and characters are not displaced from the center of interest.[16]

The supernaturalistic conception of Becket's role presents its difficulties, then, for the dramatist. But it is only one way in which the Christian significance of the subject can be presented. One can imagine an approach to the story in Christian humanist terms, as indeed to the death of Jeanne d'Arc or the Passion of Christ. Here grace in its dogmatic sense would not be imposed upon the subject, but the grace of God would be seen to emerge from the elements of situation and character—a grace that is not absolute, and a nature that is not supernature, but which would then be all the more truly dramatic and relevant.

Such an interpretation of grace is essentially Protestant, not perhaps in the Reformation sense but in the modern liberal sense. We are to suppose that Eliot ignored it or rejected it as a basis for his play because of his Anglo-Catholic theological preferences. That may not be as clear as it appears. It is possible that the dogmatic supernaturalism that underlies *Murder in the Cathedral* seemed dictated by exception for this particular drama. It is to be noted that Eliot's profound study of sin and expiation in *The Family Reunion* is carried out in nondogmatic terms. The total impression of Eliot's work suggests that while his chosen theological affiliation may be Catholic, his deeper personal debts and insights are not so easily assigned. The evident eclectic quality of his literary culture points to a deeper eclecticism in his thinking.

Yet it remains true that Eliot has taken his decision

[16] Does not *Green Pastures* conform to the proper sense of tragedy just because the "Lawd" is after all finite?

among possible alternatives and aligned himself with historical Christianity in one of its more institutional and dogmatic branches. For a modern artist or thinker to remand himself to the Catholic tradition is not the stultification so many of Eliot's critics have supposed. It was an act of profound humility and grew out of a momentous experience of the charities of life as anyone can recognize in reading *The Hollow Men* and *Ash Wednesday*. Some of his critics have not yet perhaps toiled all night and taken nothing or launched out into the same deep, or they would be better oriented in his accents. Moreover, Eliot has the same large freedom in his church that Mauriac, Claudel and Maritain have in theirs, indeed more.

Yet in becoming a Catholic or an Anglo-Catholic a man of today still leaves unsolved, for himself and for those he would lead, the more crucial personal issues of Christianity in the modern world. Especially a man like Eliot who from outside the church has known its short-comings and the unbridged gulf between it and the world, and has known the undeniable values of the secular mind, must feel demands upon his thought and action of which the hooded dogmatist is unaware. And nothing seems clearer from the main movement of modern life than that the great solutions of contemporary ethics and religion will have to come from those churches and groups that have wrestled most fearlessly and empirically with modern thought. Our age waits for Eliots who will fight it out on the exposed and hazardous front where the Protestant tradition is today reshaping itself in both theology and life, and where it is passing beyond Protestantism into something new.

CHAPTER XVIII

THE PIT FROM WHICH WE WERE DIGGED

Our aim in this final chapter is to summarize the diverse evidence that has come before us, to emphasize certain themes that have recurred, and to attempt to answer the basic question as to where we shall look for the most promising resources of imaginative creation in our culture.

The new poetry evidences a changed experience and sensibility on the part of many of our contemporaries, a change that goes deep and therefore affects spiritual and ethical attitudes. It not only calls for new arts for the present but gives promise of being a permanent and extending revolution. Some aspects and instances of this change are to be viewed as temporary and some as permanent: that is, some reflect passing moods of a particular decade or two, while others reflect deeper and more permanent transformations coming over society. Some aspects and instances are clearly regrettable, manifestations of the particular form that perennial evil takes in this particular time, a time calculated to enhance certain forms of frustration and negation. Some are auspicious, evidencing often in ambiguous ways the advent of more sensitive, more profound and more universal claims of the human spirit. These new moods are not solely "post-war." They grow out of conditions which have been partially present for a century in Western culture, but it is only recently that they have extended themselves to wide strata of society.

The conditions and factors that underlie these transformations are very complex. We have found evidence, however, for recognizing the chief factor there where much contemporary cultural history places the emphasis: the maturing in our decades of the fruits of the secularist philosophy of life, especially as it is manifested in the economic order. Capitalism has not been wholly unrestrained by religious sanctions, but what religious sanctions and controls it has had have been far from sufficient to check the dynamic drives of acquisitiveness that have worked through it as they will through any system. As a result contemporary society shows us a lack of true community, the sundering of nations, classes and individuals, and the conditions of rootlessness and insecurity that go with city and proletarian life. The consequent strifes, especially the World War and its aftermath, have disabused many men of their older patriotic and religious loyalties. At the same time the secularist philosophy of life, both influencing and influenced by these conditions, has dominated the sciences, particularly those of sociology and psychology, in such a way as to undermine what bulwarks remained to men, avowed or unconscious, in religious faith. At this point the onus rests, however, not upon science itself but upon its motives and its popularizers. And it should be borne in mind that the dissolution of existing institutions and dogmas must not all be put down on the side of loss.

The statements of the foregoing paragraph bear chiefly on the negative aspects of the change with which we are confronted. The moods evidenced by the new poetry show, however, positive qualities. There are surprising resources of community building in our world alongside those of demoralization. These must be accounted for by the stubborn persistence all through our secularizing era of resistant forces both in church and in the secular world itself, which now emerge with all the more power as the weakness of the old order becomes more manifest. It is of the first importance to scrutinize these forces and to see how far they promise as resources for the culture of the future.

The evidence we have canvassed points, finally, to a variety of spiritual quest. Our contemporaries, in these conditions excluded for the most part from traditional religious belief, that is from the Jewish-Christian tradition, find their way to some modern form of paganism. The perennial way of salvation for men, apart from this tradition, has been either some folk faith or some form of higher or lower pantheism. Today either of these alternatives means a cult of the irrational. In the one case it means for mass man the deep excitements of the collectivisms and the dark gods of soil and blood. In the other case it offers to the individual an escape from "civilization" in some form of primitivism or private Nirvana.

One of the themes which we have returned to at various points in diagnosing the regrettable aspects of the new poetry is the following. In contemporary society large numbers of men live without roots and without the natural ties that are essential for psychological health. The organic bonds with nature and the community are broken, and the primordial institution of the family is attainted. The particular significance of this for art and literature is in the effects it has upon personality. A full sense of selfhood, of mature responsible personality, is not established. Granted that such full selfhood is always a matter of degree, it is our point that with these exceptional and drastic handicaps, modern men of certain extensive groups fail to attain a full sense of reality as persons. Their experience, born of isolation and artificial conditions of life, is that of phantoms rather than of men, cyphers or "hollow men," to use Eliot's phrase. The poorest peasant has a fuller chance for the imperative elements of psychological health than one of the mass men or the sophisticated and individualistic urbanites of our society. The hallmark, as we have said, of the modernist literature, is dissociation.

From this follows a second theme. Men of this character are partly incapacitated for the deeply personalized forms of religion that we have in the Jewish and Christian traditions. They do not experience life significantly as personal relations and personal responsibility, nor can they easily be led to experience Reality or God personally. We see therefore why the religious solutions tend to be sub-personal, a retroversion either into the cult of the tribe, or into cult of the irrational powers of the unconscious. But these solutions are deeply felt as a relapse and as a seeking after strange gods, especially by those who belong to the general Puritan or at least Protestant background of the Anglo-Saxon peoples. This explains some of the peculiar features of the modernist poetry: its febrile quality, its obsession with moral questions, its blasphemy. It remains likely that the type of religion that can best save an age that inclines to these sub-personal cults is one that lays a

severe personal claim upon the individual and denies him
his too easy evasion into irresponsibility.

Where men of our time despite the influences named
achieve a sufficient stability of personality and are alienated from the orthodox religious traditions, their religious quest often takes the form of social revolution in
some form. It has been a theme of these pages that such
artists and writers are motivated, whether they acknowledge it or not, by the religious heritage of our society.
They should realize that the thoughtful and alert growing
edges of the churches and the synagogues are in deep
sympathy with them. They should see what resources are
available in purified religion for the goals they seek. It is
becoming increasingly clear that the secularized social
groups meet disappointment after disappointment as regards the disinterestedness and integrity of their leaders
and the readiness to sacrifice on the part of their rank and
file. Some of these groups are being forced to inquire
whether religious faith does not offer the resources needed
to purify of self-seeking the labor leader or the pioneer in
social projects or cooperatives. In this connection it has
also been our theme that the motives of the social revolutionary need to be analyzed more clear-sightedly than
has usually been the case. Obscure transferences of personal grievances are often at the back of what appears to
be disinterested reform. These things have been often
enough pointed out in the case of proponents of the old
order, ecclesiastical or industrial, so that their further application to the opposed group will not be resented. We
add further that the best Jewish-Christian thinking about

methods of social action now has much to contribute to the proletarians whether poets or workers.

We come to a final question approached in connection with our discussion of the problem of religious poetry today, and placed in the foreground by the study of Yeats and Eliot. In what main tradition, or to put it even more precisely, on what foundation of religion or myth or symbol, can the artist today hope best to erect any considerable work of art or literature? It is only part of the general question of the religious solution for today in terms not only of art but of life. The diversity of our poets at this point, and their relative success or failure, should give us light on the resources available today for imaginative creation, and more than that for the spiritual life generally.

It follows from our conclusion as to the momentousness of the social and aesthetic revolution of our time that the way of the traditionalist does not promise greatly. The poet working in the mood and manner of Victorian and Georgian poetry may reach a considerable number, but he will not speak for the groups who are touched by the forces that are changing the life both of the individual and society. The faiths, idealisms, and motives for the conduct of life that we associate with *The Idylls of the ·King*, with *In Memoriam*, with *The Ring and the Book*, will always have telling power for the converted. But new generations will require those insights in different accents. The particular combinations of needs, not to say satisfactions, out of which a middle-class Victorian wrote will be seen increasingly to have been *sui generis* and unrepeatable. What he found for those needs will have only partial relevance in the future. This is not to say that the values and resources of the poets of the past taken up into a new setting and felt with the new sensibility may not be used profitably again.

Another tradition that offers little promise is that of the French neo-symbolist movement, great though its influence has been among us up until quite recently in the most advanced school. This succession of writers, forced by their hostile and impervious environment to turn in upon themselves to an unprecedented degree, have sought resources for life and literature in the unconscious. Edmund Wilson has shown that in Proust and James Joyce this tradition has reached its dead end. Tate has confirmed it in the case of Hart Crane. Not that others will not go on writing in their way. But the possibilities of the method have been fully exploited. Nothing important will be done in this direction that is not either completely incomprehensible or of the nature of repetition.

We turn to ask more specifically what veins of imaginative material, what bodies of myth and symbol offer themselves as vehicles for the artist and poet who would speak to men widely. It is of interest to note that Vachel Lindsay in his lifelong warfare with the mammon and babbittry of America, especially inland America, turned up a great deal of imaginative folklore and legend for his purposes. Johnny Appleseed, the cavalier South ("The Virginians Are Coming Again"), the Negro and the Negro preacher, John Brown, even William Jennings Bryan are examples. This material is in the main, however, local and recent. The most significant symbol will always have to be more uni-

versal. Lindsay touched it in the *Congo*. It is of interest
that while this prophet-poet acknowledged himself a
Campbellite Protestant throughout his life, he does not
seem to have pressed behind his church into some firmer
grasp upon the whole Christian tradition. He used the Bible
materials but rather as an anthology on which to draw
than a decisive revelation.

It is illuminating to compare Lindsay with Walt Whitman. Both sought and found the materials for an American
legend, but Whitman gave it a more far-reaching significance by the greater total vision in which he framed it. A
poet who will launch himself far by the use of a particular
folklore or national heritage must bring it to a quasi-
religious view of man and history that lifts the mere regional sentiment to a higher significance. Here Crane and
Yeats are of interest. For Crane also wrought with American popular history and legend. In so far as he succeeded
it was because he brought to it great imaginative power.
But Crane's effective inspiration was not his vision of
America. He was a blind man to actual America as com-
pared with Whitman or even Lindsay or Sandburg. Crane's
effective inspiration was in his subjectivism and this betrayed him. Crane needed some solution of his personal
dilemma before he could make a coherent construction of
external material.

We have seen that Yeats worked a vein of Celtic lore
for many years. It was congenial to the mysticism that he
brought to it in common with other Irish poets. To this he
added a broad humanity of culture and sentiment which
lifted him above the category of regional poet, just as
Whitman was so lifted by a corresponding vision. The

insights that renewed the power of Yeats in his last years were closely related to neo-Platonic and Indian sources, not then met for the first time, however. The greatness of his work in the last period points to the importance for a poet of being steeped in some great tradition of mysticism or religious philosophy. One cannot but feel, however, that the quality of the esoteric will continue to cling to the name of even the latest Yeats. The alternative of the mystic is always open to the poet in some form, but the query remains whether in this direction poets can lay hold of material of any great generality. The frequent limitation and danger of mysticism is its individualist character. The poet here is in a case close to that of the neo-symbolists. He pays for his ivory tower by loss of a wide and nourishing participation in life. Fortunately some types of mysticism escape this danger. A Catholic mystic possesses a universal heritage. A mystic in the neo-Platonic or Indian tradition is similarly somewhat protected. But those who are first mystics and then men will always labor under a handicap as regards amplitude and humanity. Dante is the proper guide here as so often.

The case of Yeats as we have seen earlier raises the issue of Christianity in specific form. Yeats deliberated over the Christian option only to reject it. For him it connoted an asceticism that would be equivalent to a pall of darkness cast over the glowing colors of the imagination. He was both right and wrong in so thinking. This we have discussed in the chapter devoted to him. Yeats, we may hazard, was never pressed by life to the levels reported in *The Waste Land*. This poem may be taken as evidence that there are levels at which it is not possible for modern man to live at all, let alone be an artist, apart from Christianity. But beyond this, Christianity offers him a universal tradition and not an esoteric one in which to work, and in addition presents him with an unsurpassed body of symbol capable of universal appeal. The point at which Christianity meets the particular need of men today is in the overcoming of that dissociation which we have seen to be general. The Jewish-Christian tradition makes its supreme contribution to men in forcing them to accept the role of responsible selfhood in their relations to their fellows and to reality. Here all evasions into the cult of the unconscious and the irrational, however sophisticated, are forbidden. Aesthetic solution of conflict whether in the exquisite forms of Yeats' "Byzantium" or the more violent forms of Jeffers are precluded. They are all sub-personal. The artist must not win his excitement and power cheaply by abandonment of himself to the volcanic but anarchic forces of the soul. The modern instances of Baudelaire and Eliot show how adequate to extreme contemporary need is the essential katharsis of Christianity, what accesses of restorative energies are available.

There still remains the question: What form of Christianity? We have argued that for the United States at least the abiding springs of Puritanism, however covered over with sand and debris, offer the only prospect of a common cultural and spiritual rebirth, and the motives for a widely significant art and literature. In saying this we do not mean that we would turn the clock back. Protestantism deeply understood was a positive and not a negative movement. Its initial liberation was obscured from the beginning by an unconscious carry over of many uncongenial legacies from its matrix in the Middle Ages. As the Reformation took form in the sixteenth century its original creative insights accommodated themselves at a cost to the characteristics of the peoples that it had won over. What we call Puritanism with an intent to depreciate was really one half medievalism and one half Anglo-Saxon paganism. But the original impulse of the Reformation is not to be minimized or misunderstood.

The point to notice in the Reformation is its rediscovery of one of the essential truths of the New Testament, more or less inevitably lost sight of in the conditions of feudal Christendom, that of the paradoxical liberty of the individual soul. Here was the element of emancipation that explains most adequately the creative powers that flowed through the Protestant world. We speak of it as a paradoxical liberty because it was linked with responsibility. There were indeed elements of humanist or pagan revolt closely related to the working out of the Reformation particularly in its political aspects. But the decisive New Testament principle of autonomous responsible personality, which is in no sense anarchic or individualist, gave it its world-shaping spiritual power. It is this positive and creative germ of the Reformation and its earlier yet unalloyed impulses in the religious and cultural life to which the Protestant world of today should most naturally return for renewal. This is the rock from which we were hewn and the pit from which we were digged.

The Reformation thus understood was one of those birth hours or mutations that occur only once in a millennium in which history is riven to its depths and prodigious social and spiritual forces are released to remake the world. The barbarian hordes of Europe that the church and the empire had had to discipline through a long tutelage came finally to a degree of maturity. They had reached that same point that Paul's mixed Jewish and Gentile converts had reached when, referring especially to the older covenant and the Jewish law, he spoke of them as now in the status of sons rather than bond servants. It was as though at long last God said to the soul of Western man,

per ch' io te sopra te corono e mitrio,

"wherefore I crown thee king and do ordain thee priest over thyself" (*Purgatorio* xxvii, 142). Therewith God placed the translated Bible in its printed form in their hands. The new responsibility and the new liberty struck fire from the granite of the German and the Anglo-Saxon character. Inexhaustible energies were awakened in every sphere of activity. In particular the moral and political consciousness of the Anglo-Saxon people were shaped. The impulse ran through generations in England raising up one spiritual movement after another with its consequences in English society and particularly in America. To the colonies the Puritan and Separatist came aflame with eschatological dreams and continent-building momentum.

It is true that the original Reformation impulses have long grown weak. What we have of the older world-shaping vision and apocalyptic of the founders is now to a large extent a tangled residue of negations and mediocrities. The asceticism and single-mindedness which once was part of a dizzy and glorious creative movement is today, when the original great breath is gone, only inhibition and dearth of charity. But the wells which Abraham and Lot once dug and which became silted over, were dug again by their descendants generations later. So the springs which most profoundly fed Britain at the beginning of its great era and the American people in its birth hours can be the only one suitable to our later thirsts.

It is true that if we consider the present scene superficially we may well doubt if widely significant and sustained literature and art are possible in the Puritan tradition. Protestantism appears to have little symbolism. The wealth of Biblical imaginative material that Milton used has lost the place and prestige today that it once had with the reading public. One would be tempted to say that not only has the Bible lost its place in the affections of men but that this is only one aspect of the definitive loss of hold of the tradition itself. And thus we should perhaps not be surprised to note that when Mr. Eliot, of New England inheritance and temperament, found a satisfying religious mode for both life and literature it was Anglo-Catholic. We would then be led to conclude from his case and that of E. A. Robinson that a poet of the Puritan tradition, caught profoundly in the stresses of contemporary experience, if he is to go on to distinctive affirmation, must pass beyond the tradition in which he was reared. Robinson remained in a detached relation to his tradition, in a courageous Stoicism first cousin to a dour and granite Calvinism, but failed of magnificent affirmation. Eliot found it, witness the closing chorus of the Becket play, by giving himself to a deeper and older channel of Christian faith.

The outcome in the cases of Robinson and Eliot does

not prove the barrenness of the Protestant or Puritan tradition. It does indeed corroborate the indications that this tradition needs to be explored and appropriated at a deeper level. Where actual contemporary Protestantism takes unlovely forms we may recognize the infiltration of "the world" either in desiccated moralism or in bourgeois self-sufficiency. Reaction from these toward any deeper spiritual tradition is understandable. But essential Puritanism and essential Protestantism still exist. They carry in themselves the unique liberating principle of the Reformation. They therefore trace to the New Testament and the earliest church. There is no deeper and older channel of Christian faith. To it belongs whatever wealth of historic symbolism the church has gathered about itself when it has remained true to itself.

The true succession of the Reformation principle lies then with the churches of the Puritan and Dissenter tradition, whatever their short-comings. These forms of Christianity have better maintained the principle of separation of church and state and church and world. As we have said, they have wrestled most fearlessly and empirically with modern thought. There are especially two fields of thought today where modern man must insist on nondogmatic approach. One is the field of science, and here the topics of sociology and psychology are most pressing. The other is the field of social action. The thinkers and theologians of liberal Protestantism are the only ones capable of a complete realism in these urgent areas.

The character of the American people and in a lesser degree the whole Anglo-Saxon race has received its ultimate cast and temper from the great baptism of the sixteenth century. Scratch an Anglo-Saxon and you find a Calvinist. This temper moreover has communicated itself to the whole of American life, despite the diversity of its racial strains. In the deeper sense this means that our future religious solutions will be in line, not indeed with the systematic Calvinism of the sixteenth century nor the rigidified Calvinism of the seventeenth and following centuries, but with the essential Puritan and Christian discovery of autonomous and responsible personality. This has implications for political and social life that are of the utmost promise. Only in such a tradition can we have guarantees of liberty of conscience and of general civil liberties, guarantees springing from the very essence of the religious position. But if this is true of our basic religious make-up we have the answer to the question about the most potent and promising resources for art and literature. The classical Christian tradition, in those aspects that convey its best insights, with all the wealth of Biblical, artistic and literary symbol that have grown out of it, offer us what we seek.

APPENDIX

ORIENTATION AND READING GUIDE

ORIENTATION AND READING GUIDE

The following notes on the new developments in poetry and criticism will perhaps assist those to whom the poets and their work are unfamiliar. We have selected only the more important names and those least likely to be known to readers better acquainted with more traditional poets. We have also indicated a certain amount of reading in the various cases. A more complete bibliography follows and full titles of books mentioned in these notes will be given there.

1. *The Background: French Symbolism.* Much of the new poetry stems from this influence, but there is little in English poetry of the nineteenth century that can be used to describe it. The chief names that belong here are those of Baudelaire, Rimbaud, Verlaine, Mallarmé and Laforgue. Poe had an important influence on this group. Symbolism in France appears most clearly as a "second flood of the romantic movement." Just as the romantic poets in England and France revolted against the eighteenth-century classicism, so this group revolted against the new classicism in France of the Parnassians. The emphasis of the romantic poets was on the individual. They justified his free and untrammeled expression against institutions and traditional forms. The symbolist movement carried this farther, by degrees. Its final features may be stated as follows: (1) Language should be used in poetry not for literal and explicit statement but for suggestion, intimation, evocation, incantation. (2) The poet is concerned with unusual, strange or delicate moods, with special nuances of the experience of the soul, with states of consciousness. (3) Poetry should be made to approximate as closely as possible

to music or to the dream, rather than to the rational and logical. The later symbolists were in the main men who turned away from society and to introspection. The new concern of psychology following Hartmann, Charcot, Janet and finally Freud has made more deliberate and significant their revolt from the rational element in consciousness. It can be understood that the symbolists wrote a difficult poetry often in so far as the movement of their thought was that of free association of ideas or of dream sequence rather than logical sequence. It was their conviction that very significant explorations of the soul were possible in this way never before attempted. The dominant figures of contemporary or recent literature, Proust, James Jocye, T. S. Eliot, Valéry, Hart Crane, Yeats, have all been profoundly shaped by the symbolists.

This school in its relation to recent poetry is well described in relatively brief compass in Mary M. Colum's *From These Roots*, Chap. XI, pp. 312-360 ("The Revolt"). The reader is advised, however, to follow the more detailed account in Edmund Wilson's *Axel's Castle*, reading at least Chapter I on symbolism and Chapter VI ("Axel and Rimbaud").

2. *The American Background.* American poetry became highly interesting and diversified in the second decade of this century. Some of the best work or earliest work of Vachel Lindsay, Edgar Lee Masters, Carl Sandburg, Robert Frost, E. A. Robinson, Amy Lowell, Hilda Doolittle, John Gould Fletcher, Ezra Pound, Conrad Aiken and T. S. Eliot came out about this time. From various points of view one can find interpretations of this period in the following four books of special ability: Conrad Aiken, *Skepticisms: Notes on Contemporary Poetry* (1919); Amy Lowell, *Tendencies in Modern American Poetry* (1917); Louis Untermeyer, *The New Era in American Poetry* (1919); Harriet Monroe, *Poets and Their Art* (1926). Most American readers of poetry are familiar with this stage in modern poetry: free verse, with its revolt against conventional forms, and imagism with its varied demand for economy, purity and aesthetic values. Louis Unter-

meyer's anthology, *Modern American Poetry,* in its earlier editions (1919, 1921, etc.,) covers the work of this period, and it is well known what a part Miss Monroe's *Poetry, A Magazine of Verse* had in nourishing this renaissance.

Already in this period the influence of the French symbolists was beginning to be felt. After 1918 a number of new factors entered into the picture: the personal influence of individuals like Pound, Eliot, D. H. Lawrence as well as Hopkins and Owen (see below), but also more deeply the changing cultural forces. Conrad Aiken's anthology, *Modern American Poets* (1922), presents the progressive work of this period. Still later came the specific concern with social problems. Mr. Rodman's *A New Anthology of Modern Poetry* (1938) includes this as well as representative English poets of the modern groups. It will become evident that the new poetry cannot be described solely in national terms.

3. *The English Background.* Recent years have brought about a considerable change in the estimates of English poetry in the nineteenth century and the beginning of the twentieth. The reaction against rhetoric (so-called, yet with difficulty distinguished from power), the re-emphasis on Elizabethan poetry and on the seventeenth-century metaphysical poets, and the effect of the war moods, have led to a relative depreciation of Tennyson and Browning and even of the great romantic poets in England. The poets of the nineties like Wilde, Dowson and Francis Thompson suffered first. The Georgians who succeeded them were marked by a greater naturalness, but are felt to have lacked strength. They turned to nature or ships (Davies, Masefield), or were studious poets (Binyon, Abercrombie, Bridges), or were chiefly appealing for their perfection of form (A. E. Housman, de la Mare). In any case the tide turned even against the most original of them, as it did against Hardy, Kipling and the Irish poets. It is true that Yeats and Bridges have escaped the general depreciation, and even some of the others to a lesser extent.

238 THE SPIRITUAL ASPECTS OF THE NEW POETRY

The period after 1918 saw the influence of G. M. Hopkins, Wilfred Owen, and the American poets, Pound and Eliot.

Gerard Manley Hopkins, a Jesuit, died a young man in 1889. His poems were first published, with a few exceptions, in 1918. His temper and topic and often the intricacy of his language remind us of another Catholic poet, Francis Thompson. But it was the combination of his power with his technical innovations that interested the new generation. He was so successful in using unwonted rhythms, in breaking from the requirements of numerical rhythm, that he excited his readers to a freer utterance. See an excellent account of his life and work, G. F. Lahey, *Gerard Manley Hopkins* (1930).

Wilfred Owen died in France in 1918, the finest of the war poets. His accent is different from that of Rupert Brooke by its greatness of mood, its compassion, and with these the conversational quality of the style. Here was an example of how a poet could lend himself to the necessities of public events without ceasing to be a poet, and the younger English poets today, concerning themselves with politics, find in him therefore one of their "ancestors," to use their own phrase.

For an interpretation of the English background by one of the most recent English poets, see the essay *A Hope for Poetry,* written in 1934 by C. Day Lewis and published in his *Collected Poems, 1929-1933,* where it occupies almost one hundred pages. W. B. Yeats gives his account in the Introduction to his *Oxford Book of Modern Verse* (1936). Wilfred Gibson, from the point of view of the traditionalists, writes on "Contemporary English Poetry" in a careful treatment in *The University of Toronto Quarterly,* October, 1936.

4. *William Butler Yeats.* Yeats was born in Dublin in 1865 and died in 1939. In his career as a poet one can see reflected most of the changes that have come over the art in this period. His own background in youth was that of the Pre-Raphaelites and romantics. He came under the influence of the symbolists in Mallarmé's gatherings in Paris. Whether as poet or dramatist Yeats wrote for many years as a devotee of Irish legend and

folklore. His most characteristic and widely quoted poems, like those of Æ, are made up of dream and revery. About the time of the war he became more concrete. He had long had an active part in the Abbey Theatre and in the cultural movement in Ireland. His great prestige with younger writers right up until the present was due to his ability to transcend his early romanticism. It is the work of *The Tower* (1928) and *The Winding Stair and Other Poems* (1933) that we have mainly referred to in our chapter above. The section devoted to Yeats in *Axel's Castle* by Edmund Wilson is perhaps the best short treatment available. The reader will find interesting comment there, moreover, on Yeats' absorption in topics bordering on astrology and spiritism.

5. *D. H. Lawrence.* Lawrence was born in Nottinghamshire, in 1885, the son of a miner. Brought up among the workers in the collieries he found his way into teaching and writing. His first book was published when he was thirty-six. Soon after this he gave up teaching and lived entirely by his writing, in the main abroad except during the war. *Sons and Lovers,* his greatest novel, was published in 1913. The next year he married Frieda, Baroness von Richthofen. Their life in Italy, in Sardinia, Australia, Taos, N. M., furnished the background for much of his writing. They returned to Europe in 1925. He died in southern France in 1930. A number of his books had their difficulties with the censor. "Nothing seems to have grown so clearly out of fashion in a few short years as Lawrence's specific lectures on sex and obscenity. Today they seem to have gone to the same place reserved in memory for the events of early post war Europe and America."[1] Yet the treatment of these topics in his novels and poems raises issues both of censorship and of the conduct of life which deserve continued dispassionate study. Lawrence's approach to these matters was conditioned by his reaction against the faulty attitudes that handicapped his own youth, and was a basic part

---

[1] Horace Gregory: "D. H. Lawrence: The Posthumous Reputation," in Zabel, *Literary Opinion in America,* p. 512.

of his philosophy of life, somewhat dealt with in Chapter XIII above.

This author's poetry can best be understood as autobiographical notation. Lawrence was not influenced directly by symbolism, or by any other particular tradition with the exception of imagism. It is helpful to compare him with Walt Whitman. He avowedly sought inspiration and the gifts of his demon and was relatively unconcerned as to perfection of form in the usual sense. He also coveted for himself the role of teacher or prophet. His peculiar intuitive powers are well exhibited in an early prose book, *Twilight in Italy* (1916). It is Lawrence as a person and as a type significant for our age (i.e., by reaction) that most deserves attention. For this see *The Letters of D. H. Lawrence*, edited and with an Introduction by Aldous Huxley; also, *A Poet and Two Painters*, by Knud Merrild.

6. *Ezra Pound.* Mr. Pound, an American born in Idaho, began in the imagist group. He was even more versatile than Amy Lowell in canvassing the suggestions that might be found for the poet's art in foreign literatures, French, Provençal, Persian, Anglo-Saxon. His interests have appeared to be strictly aesthetic. Becoming an expatriate he has had a primary role in stimulating new developments everywhere, more perhaps by personal contact than by his own writing. Yet some of his earlier work in *Personae* (1909) and especially his poem *Hugh Selwyn Mauberley* (1920) evidence his ability to stand with the first in the succeeding phases of poetic method. During the last fifteen years he has been publishing an unfinished work, the *Cantos*, a production of extraordinary character, both for its omniscience, its wit, its difficulty and its occasional passages of classic perfection. In the *Cantos* as in *Mauberley* Pound shows the characteristics that appear in Eliot and other moderns. The present-day world is set off against the greatness of the past by the use of classical allusions. At the same time by the use of such themes or myths as those of Odysseus or Dionysus life today is seen in universal

terms. Uninitiated readers may be referred to the anthologies for samples of his work, but they are not likely to appreciate his significance apart from some fuller knowledge of the modern poetry movement as a whole. Some indication of his influence is found in the fact that T. S. Eliot dedicates *The Waste Land* to him as *il miglior fabbro* (Dante's tribute to Virgil, the "better craftsman"). As to his philosophy of life, Yeats has written, "Ezra Pound has made flux his theme; plot, characterization, logical discourse, seem to him abstractions unsuitable to a man of his generation." We must add to this, however, the observation that Pound appears in his most significant work as a moralist, especially in a recurrent theme in the *Cantos*: "usura contra natura," i.e., an indictment of the acquisitive motive in the modern world under the symbol of usury.

7. *Thomas Stearns Eliot.* Born in St. Louis in 1888, Eliot was of New England background. He graduated from Harvard in 1909 and studied in Paris and Oxford. He has lived in England in the main and became a British subject in 1927. He founded the *Criterion* in London in 1922 and has edited it until its demise in 1939. Eliot has had a profound influence as a literary critic. He has brought to English criticism a breadth of acquaintance with other literatures and a seriousness which have inevitably led to a devaluation of the impressionism that prevailed before. As a result there has been a considerable revision of values in estimating the chief figures of English literature. Eliot's prose style is lucid and in the finest tradition. As regards his poetry, his volume *Prufrock* (1917) showed the influence of the French symbolists, especially Laforgue, and has much of the difficulty or startling character indicated in connection with their work. Laforgue was notable for his ironic commentary on the world, his mixing of colloquial and severe, of sordid and great. Eliot carries these themes on to a powerful expression in *Poems* (1920). In the poem "Gerontion" in this collection we have an old man in sordid conditions tormented by the undecided issues of his life, who, in interior monologue, by passing reflections, gives us an

agonizing sense of life's ambiguities in the moral realm. See above, page 171. Sweeney in these same poems is a character in whom Eliot contrasts the vulgarity of modern life with greatness in the past. *The Waste Land* (1922) takes its symbolism from the legend of the Holy Grail. Here we have a sterile land and all its life and inhabitants cursed with drouth and impotence. The poet has in mind our contemporary culture with its impersonality, its dearth of spirit, the vulgarity of its pleasures, its smothered impulses. The drouth and thirst point ultimately toward a religious satisfaction. The difficulty of the poem arises out of the symbolist method and the many references to older literature and scripture. The poem is best read with the help of some introduction like that in Chapter IV of *Axel's Castle*, or better a commentary like that of F. R. Leavis in *New Bearings in English Poetry*. Eliot's poem *Ash Wednesday* (1930) continues the theme of spiritual struggle in a similar method. In 1928 this writer tentatively stated his position as classicist in literature, Anglo-Catholic in religion, and royalist in politics. He has written on ecclesiastical themes and took part in the Ecumenical Conference of the Churches at Oxford in 1937. His verse plays, *Murder in the Cathedral* and *The Rock*, were written for special occasions, the former having been first produced at Canterbury Cathedral. Many readers will perhaps do well to begin their reading of Eliot with the first of these plays. His essay on Dante is specially recommended also. The last work to appear is the verse play *Family Reunion* (1938). Reading: Edmund Wilson, *Axel's Castle*, Chap. IV; Leavis, as above; F. O. Matthiessen, *The Achievement of T. S. Eliot;* H. R. Williamson, *The Poetry of T. S. Eliot.*

8. *Conrad Aiken.* Born in Georgia in 1889, a graduate of Harvard, 1911, poet, novelist, critic and anthologist, Mr. Aiken has lived in Massachusetts until 1921 and thereafter until lately in Sussex, England. He may be classed as one of the psychological poets with Eliot and MacLeish. Eliot, Aiken and Gertrude Stein reacted strongly to the psychological topics and

experiments of their student days at Harvard at about the same time. Aiken has always showed a marked lyrical gift, but his best work has been in the themes of introspection exemplified in the poems we have discussed in the section devoted to him above. A very interesting introduction to his work is available in Houston Peterson's *The Melody of Chaos* (1931). Aiken's critical principles as evident in his excellent volume *Skepticisms* (1919) as well as his modern anthology show a mind very exacting and judicious. At that time he pointed out the deficiencies of much free verse and noted the quality of some rising poets like Eliot who were then generally ignored.

9. *Archibald MacLeish.* This poet was born in Illinois in 1892. He took degrees at Yale and Harvard, the latter in law. He served as Captain in the Field Artillery in France. He has been identified with journalism if that term may be applied to *Fortune.* MacLeish's work for some time (*Streets in the Moon,* 1926; *The Hamlet of A. MacLeish,* 1928) related him to the symbolist methods and topics we have described above. At the same time his poetry of this period reflected special study of the seventeenth-century English poets and an interest in recent psychology. We have given our highest praise above to the *Hamlet.* Uninitiated readers of it will note the use of ancient myth or folklore as in Pound, Eliot and James Joyce. In *Conquistador* (1932), MacLeish deals with the conquest of Mexico in a long narrative poem of action and reminiscence. *Public Speech: Poems* (1936) and the now well-known verse plays for radio are concretely social in their subject matter. The writer has stated in articles his conviction that the poet of our time must avoid a "private speech" or a role isolated from the common life of our world, and should find himself at home in and adequate to the great issues of society. The reader will find excellent examples of the use of new methods for new themes in *Frescoes for Mr. Rockefeller's City* (1933), or one of the radio plays, such as *The Fall of the City* (1937). The poet's own statement of his principles in these later books may be read in the *Yale Review,* Vol. 27, No. 3 (1938), Public

244 THE SPIRITUAL ASPECTS OF THE NEW POETRY

Speech and Private Speech in Poetry," and in the *Atlantic Monthly*, June, 1939.

10. *Hart Crane*. See special note above, p. 122.

11. *Robinson Jeffers*. Mr. Jeffers was born in 1887 in Pennsylvania. His college study was in southern California, and he has spent most of his life at Carmel in that state, living in a stone tower that looks out over Monterey Bay. Jeffers' most characteristic work is in the form of extended dramatic narratives in free verse, marked by violence of subject matter and power of treatment. Their interest lies rather in the detail and the mystical background than in the narratives as such. As we have said in the chapter devoted to him, Jeffers' poems indicate an abhorrence for human living in its empirical situation, and it is in the theme of its salvation, man's surpassing himself, in some form of mystical achievement, that the writing receives its power. It is difficult to relate Jeffers to particular influences or traditions. He has used the themes of the Greek tragedies and the life of Christ, and it is evident that he writes with modern psychological insights in mind. Readers will find his *The Tower Beyond Tragedy* (in *The Women at Point Sur*, 1927), based on the Orestes theme, or *Give Your Hearts to the Hawks* (1933) or *Cawdor* (1928) among the best examples of his work. Those disorientated by the longer poems will find much of his best quality in the shorter ones. Mr. Yvor Winters' negative treatment of Jeffers will be found in his *Primitivism and Decadence*, pp. 16-20.[2] Book length studies of the poet include those of George Sterling, *Robinson Jeffers: the Man and the Artist* (1926), and L. C. Powell, *Robinson Jeffers, the Man and His Work* (1934).

12. *W. H. Auden and the group associated with him*. W. H. Auden, Stephen Spender, C. Day Lewis, Louis MacNeice, Charles Madge and others form the most recent group of English poets, one that not only has its own characteristics, but which has succeeded in awakening a wider interest in poetry. These men were born between 1904 and 1910 and in most

[2] At fuller length in Zabel, *Literary Opinion in America*, pp. 245 ff.

cases were at Oxford together. They have been identified with the review *New Verse* edited by Geoffrey Grigson. Many of the influences described above find expression in their work but they have first of all been identified as poets concerned with society and politics of a left-wing position. Those that identify themselves as communists are philosophical rather than proletarian converts.

These men while they are grateful to Lawrence, T. S. Eliot, Yeats and Pound acknowledge more particularly the technical influence of Hopkins and the spiritual influence of Owen. Yeats sees three elements combined in them, a modern vocabulary, a sharp accuracy of observation, and "a sense of suffering no longer passive." This group, while they vary greatly as regards their actual political credo, yet by their revolutionary ardor and vitality contrast sharply with the Waste Land mood of their seniors. With the early thirties their poems, satires, plays, novels brought a new note into the English scene. New magazines sprang up; new anthologies were published. The social and international scene found its way into literature, and soon some of the group were taking an active hand in Spain on the side of the loyalists.

Much of their work has been in the form of satire upon English or European society, as a world going to pieces. They evoke brilliantly the mediocrity or irresponsibility of various strata in British life. They see the effects of town civilization, the expansion of the social unit to the point where "personal life is attenuated and dissipated." Day Lewis notes the handicaps to poetry that are found in shallow education, the mass publicity of radio and cinema, the cheap novel, the "scientific dope." All this means that the poets to preserve their own integrity must unite on their own ground and hold to their own values and terms, even if this means a degree of obscurity in their work for those outside. Yet no school has been more colloquial in its use of "public speech" and public vocabulary.

Of these poets, W. H. Auden has received the most attention. His work is chiefly a powerful exposure of modern ills in various tenor all the way from lampooning to prophecy. There is a frequent use of psychological symbols which makes for depth and difficulty. The reader unfamiliar with this group would do well to approach Auden or the others through an introduction like that of Day Lewis in his essay, *A Hope for Poetry* (1934). He will find representative poems of these writers in the anthologies of Yeats and Rodman. He may then read *The Orators* in Auden's *Poems* (1934) or one of the extravaganza plays, *The Dog Beneath the Skin* or *The Ascent of F6*, both written by Auden in collaboration with Isherwood. Spender is the most lyrical of the group. His critical volume, *The Destructive Element* (1935) well describes the roots of the new movement, and in the last chapter interprets the work of Auden with some detail. For an example of Day Lewis' verse let the inquirer take the series "From Feathers to Iron" in *Collected Poems, 1929-1933*. This sequence deals with the anticipated and realized birth of the poet's first child and illustrates both the method and the social views of the group.

13. *A note on some of the newer critics mentioned.* Literary criticism has reflected the same new forces in the post-war world that have determined much of the poetry. On the one hand there has been concern with social and political realities as underlying all artistic expression. Much of the best recent criticism has come from left-wing periodicals like the *Nation, New Republic, Dial, Hound and Horn*. Again, the interest in more exact aesthetic criteria has been fostered by closer contact with French criticism. Altogether there has been a new severity in judging our traditional culture and poetry, based on a wider acquaintance with the world's literature, on social analysis and on psychological study. The older school of criticism represented by Saintsbury and the humanists are disparaged as impressionistic. They were men of taste who judged literature as a tea taster judges tea. They knew what they liked but hardly knew why they liked it, nor could they do justice to moods or methods outside their limited scope. Their work had a good deal of the arbitrary about it; their

appreciation took the form of unsystematic judgments by men often indeed of distinguished culture. The younger critics have sought to base their appreciation on more objective analysis.

For American work since the war the reader is referred to a collection of critical essays brought together and introduced by M. D. Zabel, *Literary Opinion in America* (1937), where fifty papers by thirty writers are reprinted covering most aspects of modernist literature. He will find there a valuable *Introduction* by the editor, and an illuminating set of appendices in the form of bibliographies and notes on the writers. Many important contemporary critics not alluded to in this present study will be found represented there, such as J. W. Krutch, Marianne Moore, Kenneth Burke, Malcolm Cowley, Horace Gregory.

The following names have been more particularly alluded to above, or have been of particular help to the present author. (Criticism by the poets Aiken, Day Lewis, Eliot, Spender has been referred to in the sections just above.)

R. P. Blackmur was born in Massachusetts in 1904. As poet and critic he was one of the editors of the advanced critical review, *The Hound and Horn,* founded in Cambridge (Massachusetts), in 1927. He received a Guggenheim Fellowship in 1937. His volume of criticism *"The Double Agent: Essays in Craft and Elucidation"* (1935) is one of the ablest technical studies of modernist literature and of the task of the critic. Papers will be found on E. E. Cummings, Ezra Pound, T. S. Eliot and others.

John Crowe Ransom was born in Tennessee in 1888 and studied at Vanderbilt University and Oxford. He has taught at Vanderbilt since 1914. He received a Guggenheim Fellowship in 1931. He has belonged to the group commonly spoken of as the "southern agrarians" which also includes Allen Tate, a group distinctly interested in cultural as well as aesthetic matters. Ransom has written several volumes of poetry and at least two volumes of criticism, including the more recent and

important *The World's Body* (1938). In this book by the study
of poets old and new Mr. Ransom makes some interesting
points. His title signifies that poetry should give us not what
science gives us, the abstractions of the world, but the world
itself. Another outstanding theme, on the conservative side here
as regards technique, is a warning against the common types
of romantic lyricism. He pleads for the depersonalizing of
the artist's materials. The artist should don a mask, that is, he
should use traditional patterns in some sense to give a greater
universality to his private experience. Mr. Ransom is now
teaching at Kenyon College in Ohio, where he edits *The
Kenyon Review*, a quarterly founded in 1938.

Laura Riding and Robert Graves are English poets and
critics who belonged in the early post-war years to the Free
Verse school in their respective ways. The poetry of each of
them has only recently appeared in a somewhat definitive
collection and has been highly approved. In 1929 they published jointly *A Survey of Modernist Poetry*. This is an extremely able and interesting discussion of the experimental
poets of our time. It is not a popular book. It deals with some
of the most difficult of the new poets. The authors attempt to
justify much of this work in the eyes of "the plain reader."
The faults of imagism, free verse, Georgian poetry, are
pointed out and emphasis is placed on exactness and pre-
cision of observation, on freedom from rhetoric, on detachment
on the part of the poet and on intellectual content.

Allen Tate is grouped with the southern agrarians, and he
and Mr. Ransom exchange compliments in the dedications or
prefaces of their critical work. He was born in Virginia in
1899 and attended Vanderbilt University. He is the author of
biographies of Stonewall Jackson and Jefferson Davis. His
four volumes of poetry include perhaps the most notable, *The
Mediterranean and Other Poems* (1936). He has had a leading
part in the cultural and critical discussions in the South as
editor, teacher and essayist. He is concerned with the conflict
of an old cultural tradition, in particular that of the South,

with modern demoralization. He has an aristocratic view of the arts. "Poetry is the art of apprehending and concentrating our experience in the mysterious limitation of form." Yet for all his insistence on the best tradition Mr. Tate's own poetry is that of so extremely cultivated and subtle and modern a mind that it is by no means easy for "the plain reader." His outlook may be well studied in the essay "Three Types of Poetry" in the volume *Reactionary Essays on Poetry and Ideas* (1936).

Edmund Wilson was born in New Jersey in 1895 and took his college work at Princeton where he graduated in 1916. He has been identified with a number of the progressive reviews, especially the *New Republic* of which he was the literary editor from 1926 to 1931. He has written poetry, imaginative prose, social and literary criticism. His interest in literature bears specially upon its relation to cultural and social backgrounds. His volume *Axel's Castle, A Study of the Imaginative Literature of 1870 to 1930* (1931) is perhaps the outstanding work in this country on the backgrounds and significance of modernist literature. The book deals with Eliot, Yeats, Joyce, Proust and others in their background in the French symbolist tradition. The thesis of the book is that modern civilization has driven the artist into the ivory tower of subjectivism, the extreme limit being reached in these men. His book is both a criticism of poetry and of society.

Yvor Winters was born in Chicago in 1900. He took his doctorate in Stanford University where he has held a chair in English literature. Both a poet and a critic, he has contributed to many of the progressive reviews. *Primitivism and Decadence: A Study of American Experimental Poetry* (1937) gathers up much of his best work. Winters is interested in an exact analysis of the poetic process, and in finding a precise terminology in this field, and then in applying it to the so-called unintelligibility or nonrational aspects of modern poetry. While appreciative of the new work he points out the faults both of method and morale in these poets.

BIBLIOGRAPHY

The following bibliography includes all works mentioned in the book. It is divided into three sections: A. Criticism and biography; B. Poets (together with a few titles mentioned in the fields of fiction and drama); C. Anthologies. A certain number of titles in each of these categories have been added to the list of those actually cited or referred to in the text, but the bibliography does not pretend to be exhaustive.

A. CRITICISM, BIOGRAPHY, LETTERS

Aiken, Conrad, *Skepticisms: Notes on Contemporary Poetry.* New York: Knopf, 1919.

Berdiaeff, Nicholas, *Un nouveau moyen age.* Paris: Plon, 1933. English translation, *The End of Our Time.* New York: Sheed, 1933.

——, *Esprit et liberté.* Paris: Editions "Je sers," 15 rue du Four, 1933. English translation, *Liberty and the Spirit.* New York: Scribner, 1935.

Blackmur, R. P., *The Double Agent.* New York: Arrow Editions, 1935.

Brooks, Cleanth, *Modern Poetry and the Tradition.* University of No. Carolina Press, 1939.

Coffin, R. P. T., *New Poetry of New England: Frost and Robinson.* Baltimore: Johns Hopkins, 1938.

Colum, Mary M., *From These Roots, The Ideas That Have Made Modern Literature.* New York: Scribner, 1937.

Cowley, Malcolm (editor), *After the Genteel Tradition; American Writers Since 1910.* New York: 1937.

Day Lewis, C. *A Hope for Poetry.* In *Collected Poems.* New York: Random, 1935.

Drew, Elizabeth, *Discovering Poetry.* New York: Norton, 1935.

Eliot, T. S., *Selected Essays, 1917-1932.* New York: Harcourt, 1932.

——, *The Use of Poetry and the Use of Criticism.* Cambridge: Harvard University Press, 1933.

——, *Essays Ancient and Modern*. New York: Harcourt, 1936.

Every, Brother George, Article: "Life, Life, Eternal Life." In *The Student World* (Geneva, Switzerland), vol. 31, no. 2 (Spring 1938).

Figgis, Darrell, *Æ (George W. Russell)*. New York: Dodd, Mead, 1916.

Gibson, Wilfred, Article: "Contemporary English Poetry." In *The University of Toronto Quarterly*, vol. 6, no. 1 (October 1936).

Hicks, Granville, and Others, *Proletarian Literature in the United States: an Anthology*. New York: International Publishers, 1935.

Hillyer, Robert, *Some Roots of English Poetry*. Norton, Massachusetts: Wheaton College Press, 1933.

Horton, Philip, *Hart Crane, The Life of an American Poet*. New York: Norton, 1937.

Huxley, Aldous, "Introduction" to *The Letters of D. H. Lawrence*. New York: Viking, 1932.

James, D. G., *Skepticisms and Poetry*. London: Allen and Unwin, 1937.

Jones, H. M., "The Drift to Liberalism in the American Eighteenth Century." In *Authority and the Individual*. Cambridge: Harvard University Press, 1937, pp. 319-348.

Jung, C. G., *Psychology and Religion*. New Haven: Yale University Press, 1938.

Lahey, G. F., *Gerard Manley Hopkins*. London: Milford, 1930.

Lawrence, D. H., *The Letters of*, Edited by Aldous Huxley. New York: Viking, 1932.

Lawrence, Frieda (von Richthofen), *"Not I, but the wind."* New York: Viking, 1934.

Leavis, F. R., *New Bearings in English Poetry*. London: Chatto, 1932.

Lenin, V. I., and J. Staline, *Sur la littérature et l'art*, edited by Jean Fréville. Paris: Editions sociales internationales, 1937.

——, *Religion*. New York: International Publishers, 1933.

Lewis, C. Day, *See* Day Lewis.

Lowell, Amy, *Tendencies in Modern American Poetry*. New York: Macmillan, 1917.

Lowes, John Livingston, *Convention and Revolt in Poetry*. Boston: Houghton Mifflin, 1919.

Luccock, H. E., *Contemporary American Literature and Religion.* Chicago: Willett, Clark, 1934.

MacIver, R. M., "The Historical Pattern of Social Change." In *Authority and the Individual.* (Harvard Tercentenary Publications), Cambridge: 1937, pp. 126-153.

MacLeish, Archibald, Article: "Public Speech and Private Speech in Poetry." *The Yale Review,* vol. 27, no. 3 (Spring 1938), pp. 534-537.

——, Article: "In Challenge not Defense." *Poetry, A Magazine of Verse,* vol. LII, no. IV (July 1938).

——, Article: "Poetry and the Public World." *The Atlantic Monthly,* June 1939.

MacNeice, Louis, *Modern Poetry, A Personal Essay.* London and New York: Oxford, 1938.

Marx, Karl and d'Engels, *Sur la littérature et l'art,* edited by Jean Fréville. Paris: Editions sociales internationales, 1936.

Matthiessen, F. O., *The Achievement of T. S. Eliot.* Boston: Houghton Mifflin, 1935.

Merrild, Knud, *A Poet and Two Painters, A Memoir of D. H. Lawrence.* New York: Viking, 1938.

Monroe, Harriet, *Poets and Their Art.* New York: Macmillan, 1932.

——, *A Poet's Life.* New York: Macmillan, 1938.

Peterson, Houston, *The Melody of Chaos.* New York: Longmans, 1931.

Powell, L. C., *Robinson Jeffers, The Man and His Work.* Los Angeles: Primavera, 1934.

Ransom, J. C., *The World's Body, Foundations for Literary Criticism.* New York: Scribner, 1938.

Read, Herbert, *Poetry and Anarchism.* London: Macmillan, 1939.

Richards, I. A., *Principles of Literary Criticism.* New York: Harcourt, 1925.

——, *Science and Poetry.* London: Paul, Trench and Trubner, 1926.

——, *Practical Criticism.* New York: Harcourt, 1935.

——, *Coleridge on Imagination.* New York: Harcourt, 1935.

Riding, Laura and Robert Graves, *A Survey of Modernist Poetry.* London: Heinemann, 1929.

Roberts, Michael, *The Modern Mind.* London: Faber, 1937.

Slater, J. R., *Recent Literature and Religion*. New York: Harper, 1938.

Sparrow, John, *Sense and Poetry*. New Haven: Yale University Press, 1934.

Spender, Stephen, *The Destructive Element*. Boston: Houghton Mifflin, 1936.

——, *Forward from Liberalism*. New York: Random, 1937.

Sterling, George, *Robinson Jeffers: The Man and the Artist*. New York: Boni and Liveright, 1926.

Tate, Allen, *Reactionary Essays on Poetry and Ideas*. New York: Scribner, 1936.

Turnell, Martin, *Poetry and Crisis*. London: Sands, 1938.

Valéry, Paul, *Regards sur le monde actuel*. Paris: Stock, Delamain et Boutelleau, 1931.

Williamson, H. R., *The Poetry of T. S. Eliot*. London: Hodder & Stoughton, 1932. New York: Putnam, 1933.

Wilson, Edmund, *Axel's Castle: A Study in the Imaginative Literature of 1870-1930*. New York: Scribner, 1931.

——, *The Triple Thinkers: Ten Essays in Literature*. New York: Harcourt, Brace, 1938.

Winters, Yvor, *Primitivism and Decadence: A Study of American Experimental Poetry*. New York: Arrow Editions, 1937.

Yeats, W. B., "Introduction" to *Oxford Book of Modern Verse*. New York: Oxford, 1936.

Zabel, M. D., *Literary Opinion in America;* Essays Illustrating the Status, Methods, and Problems of Criticism in the United States Since the War, Edited with an introduction by M. D. Z. New York and London: Harper, 1937.

B. POETS

Abercrombie, Lascelles, *The Poems of*. London and New York: Oxford, 1930.

Æ (George Russell), *Collected Poems*. London and New York: Macmillan, 1917.

Agee, James, *Permit Me Voyage*. New Haven: Yale, 1934.

Aiken, Conrad, *Selected Poems*. New York: Scribner, 1933.

——, *Preludes for Memnon*. New York: Scribner, 1931.

Auden, W. H., *Poems*. New York: Random, 1934.

——, *On this Island*. New York: Random, 1937.

Auden, W. H. and C. Isherwood, *The Dog Beneath the Skin*. New York: Random, 1935.

——, *The Ascent of F6*. New York: Random, 1937.

Crane, Hart, *Collected Poems*. New York: Liveright, 1933.

Davies, W. H., *Collected Poems*. New York: Jonathan Cape, 1929.

Day Lewis, C., *Collected Poems*. New York: Random, 1935.

Eliot, T. S., *Poems 1909-1925* (including *The Waste Land*). New York: Harcourt, 1932.

——, *Ash Wednesday*. New York: Putnam, 1930.

——, *The Rock: A Pageant Play*. New York: Harcourt, 1934.

——, *Murder in the Cathedral*. New York: Harcourt, 1935.

——, *The Family Reunion*. New York: Harcourt, 1939.

Fearing, Kenneth, *Dead Reckoning*. New York: Random, 1939.

Hillyer, Robert, *A Letter to Robert Frost and Others*. New York: Knopf, 1937.

Hopkins, G. M., *Poems*. London and New York: Oxford, 1930.

Jeffers, Robinson, *Roan Stallion, Tamar and Other Poems*. New York: Random, 1925.

——, *The Women at Point Sur*. New York: Liveright, 1927.

——, *Cawdor and Other Poems*. New York: Liveright, 1928.

——, *Give Your Heart to the Hawks*. New York: Random, 1933.

Lawrence, D. H., *Collected Poems*. New York: Jonathan Cape, 1929.

——, *Last Poems*. New York: Viking, 1933.

Leonard, W. E., *A Son of Earth*. New York: Viking, 1928.

MacLeish, Archibald, *Streets in the Moon*. Boston: Houghton Mifflin, 1926.

——, *The Hamlet of A. MacLeish*. Boston: Houghton Mifflin, 1928.

——, *Poems 1924-1933*. Boston: Houghton Mifflin, 1934.

——, *Panic: A Play in Verse*. Boston: Houghton Mifflin, 1935.

——, *Public Speech: Poems*. New York: Farrar & Rinehart, 1936.

——, *The Fall of the City: A Verse Play for Radio*. New York: Farrar & Rinehart, 1937.

——, *Land of the Free*. New York: Harcourt, 1938.

——, *Air Raid: A Verse Play for Radio*. New York: Harcourt, 1938.

Millay, Edna St. V., *Conversation at Midnight*. New York: Harper, 1937.

Moore, T. Sturge, *Selected Poems*. London and New York: Macmillan, 1934.

Mukerji, D. G., *The Song of God* (translation of *The Bhagavad-Gita*). New York: Dutton, 1931.

O'Neill, Eugene, *The Great God Brown*. New York: Boni & Liveright, 1926.

Patchen, Kenneth, *Before the Brave*. New York: Random, 1936.

——, *First Will and Testament*. Norfolk, Conn.: New Directions, 1939.

Perse, St. J., *Anabase* (with a translation by T. S. Eliot). London: Faber, 1930.

Pound, Ezra, *Personae; The Collected Poems*. New York: Boni & Liveright, 1926.

——, *A Draft of XXX Cantos*. Paris: Hours Press, 1930. New York: Farrar, 1933.

Read, Herbert, *Poems, 1914-1934*. London: Faber, 1935.

Robinson, E. A., *Collected Poems*. New York: Macmillan, 1929.

——, *Amaranth*. New York: Macmillan, 1934.

Rukeyser, Muriel, *U. S. 1*. New York: Covici, Friede, 1938.

Schwartz, Delmore, *In Dreams Begin Responsibilities*. Norfolk, Conn.: New Directions, 1939.

Scott, Evelyn, *The Winter Alone* (Poems). New York: Cape, 1930.

——, *Escapade*. New York: Cape, 1933.

——, *A Calendar of Sin*. New York: Cape, 1931.

Scott, Geoffrey, *Poems*. London: Oxford, 1931.

Spender, Stephen, *Poems*. New York: Random, 1934.

——, *Vienna*. New York: Random, 1935.

——, *Trial of a Judge*. London: Faber, 1938. New York: Random, 1938.

Stephens, James, *Songs from the Clay*. London: Macmillan, 1915.

Stevens, Wallace, *The Man with the Blue Guitar*. New York: Knopf, 1937.

Tate, Allen, *The Mediterranean and Other Poems*. New York: Scribner, 1936.

Thomas, Dylan, *The World I Breathe*. Norfolk, Conn.: New Directions, 1939.

Thompson, Francis, *The Works of*. London: Burns, Oates & Washbourne, 1913 (New York: Scribner).

Valéry, Paul, *Charmes*. Paris: N. R. F., 1926.

Wilder, A. N., *Arachne: Poems*. New Haven: Yale Univ. Press, 1928.

Wilder, Charlotte, *Phases of the Moon*. New York: Coward-Mc-Cann, 1936.

——, *Mortal Sequence*. New York: Coward-McCann, 1939.

Williams, William Carlos, *The Complete Collected Poems, 1906-1938*. Norfolk, Conn.: New Directions, 1939.

Wylie, Elinor, *Angels and Earthly Creatures*. New York: Knopf, 1929.

——, *Collected Poems*. New York: Knopf, 1932.

Yeats, W. B., *Collected Poems*. New York: Macmillan, 1937.

C. ANTHOLOGIES

Abercrombie, Lascelles, *New English Poems*. London: Gollancz, 1931.

Aiken, Conrad, *Modern American Poets*. New York: Modern Library, 1927.

Anderson, G. K. and Eda Lou Walton, *This Generation:* A Selection of British and American Literature from 1914 to the Present with Historical and Critical Essays. Chicago: Scott, Foresman, 1939.

Gregory, Horace, *New Letters in America*. New York: Norton.

Hicks, Granville, and Others, *Proletarian Literature in the United States: An Anthology*. New York: International Publishers, 1935.

Lehmann, John, *New Writing*. Spring and Autumn, 1936. London: John Lane.

——, *Ibid.*, Spring and Autumn, 1937, etc. London: Lawrence & Wishart.

Monroe, Harriet and A. C. Henderson, *The New Poetry*. New York: Macmillan, 1923.

New Directions in Prose and Poetry. Norfolk, Conn.: 1936 and following years.

Pound, Ezra, *Active Anthology*. London: Faber, 1936.

Roberts, Michael, *The Faber Book of Modern Verse*. London: Faber, 1936.

Rodman, Selden, *A New Anthology of Modern Poetry*. New York: Literary Guild of America (Random), 1938.

Untermeyer, Louis, *Modern American Poetry*, Fourth Edition. New York: Harcourt, 1930.

——, *Modern British Poetry*, Third Edition. New York: Harcourt, 1930.

Woolf, L., and Virginia, *New Country;* Prose and Poetry by the Authors of *New Signatures*. London: Woolf, 1933.

——, *New Signatures; Poems by Several Hands*. London: Woolf, 1935.

Yeats, W. B., *The Oxford Book of Modern Verse, 1892-1935*. New York: Oxford, 1936.

INDEX[1]

[1] References in heavy type indicate quotations or detailed treatment.

259